BK.
4.25

FEB 7 1976

*Hawthorne's Fiction:* THE
LIGHT & THE DARK

# Hawthorne's Fiction: THE

## LIGHT & THE DARK

Richard Harter Fogle

UNIVERSITY OF OKLAHOMA PRESS

NORMAN

*By* RICHARD HARTER FOGLE

*Hawthorne's Fiction: The Light & the Dark* (Norman 1952, 1964)

*The House of the Seven Gables* (editor) (New York, 1963)

*The Idea of Coleridge's Criticism* (Berkeley, 1962)

*Eight American Writers* (editor, with others) (New York, 1962)

*Melville's Shorter Tales* (Norman, 1960)

*John Keats: Selected Poetry and Letters* (New York, 1951)

*The Imagery of Keats and Shelley* (Chapel Hill, 1949)

*Library of Congress Catalog Card Number:* 64–23334

*To my father,* JAMES U. FOGLE, *1877-1960*

# *Preface*

WORK in Hawthorne scholarship and criticism has been exceptionally interesting from the times of E. P. Whipple and George Parsons Lathrop down to the present, and I have duly drawn upon it. If it is possible to distinguish, however, I am most fully indebted to F. O. Matthiessen's *American Renaissance,* Randall Stewart's fine editions of the *English* and *American Notebooks,* and Newton Arvin's *Hawthorne.* The debt is indirect: it does not include my method of approach, and it does not involve any close agreement on the value of Hawthorne's writing.

My emphasis is primarily expository and to some extent appreciative rather than judicial, simply because I have a larger opinion of Hawthorne's worth than any critic I have encountered, with the single exception of Hyatt Howe Waggoner. If it has a fault, Hawthorne criticism can be accused of being more grudging than the situation demands, and of judging Hawthorne's art before it has been fully explained. My attitude prevents me from distinguishing the relative value of individual works; but it seems to me more useful, for example, to point out the virtues of *The Blithedale Romance* than to reassert its inferiority to *The Scarlet Letter.*

Thanks are due to the editors of *The University of Toronto Quarterly, The New England Quarterly,* and

*Hawthorne's Fiction*

*Tulane Studies in English* for permission to reprint in revised form a number of essays which appeared in these journals. I gratefully acknowledge the financial assistance from the Tulane University Council on Research which allowed me time to work on this book.

Quotations from Hawthorne's works are taken from the text of the Riverside Edition, edited by G. P. Lathrop.

RICHARD HARTER FOGLE

*New Orleans*
*June 3, 1952*

# Preface to the Revised Edition

THIS BOOK WAS, I believe, the first of its kind published on Hawthorne's fiction. Its most noteworthy successors in general method have been H. H. Waggoner's *Hawthorne: A Critical Study* (1955) and Roy R. Male's *Hawthorne's Tragic Vision* (1957), excellent books both; and perhaps Rudolph Von Abele's *The Death of the Artist: A Study of Hawthorne's Disintegration* (1955). Mr. Von Abele's purposes were, however, quite different from mine; I have had no ambition to preside over Hawthorne's disintegration, if any.

Since the first publication of *Hawthorne's Fiction* at least eleven books on him have appeared; and, as a sampling, about one hundred articles from 1955 to 1962. The "Annual Bibliography for 1962" in *Publications of the Modern Language Association* lists fifty-seven Hawthorne items. Numerous "casebooks" for Hawthorne study now exist; it may be remarked incidentally that the most recent, Elizabeth Donohue's *The Hawthorne Question*, makes ambiguity, a topic discussed here, its major theme. A new edition of our writer is being prepared at Ohio State University, and at Yale a definitive collection of his letters, under the meticulous editorship of Norman Holmes. Hawthorne, in fact, continues to be a thoroughly current author. Walter Blair's elaborate survey of Hawthorne criticism and scholarship in *Eight American Authors,* now supplemented by J. Chesley Mathews in a new edition, has made my own "Suggested Readings" superfluous, and I have accordingly dropped them from the present edition of *Hawthorne's Fiction.* This act does not constitute endorsement of Professor Blair's opinion of my work, which is considerably lower than my own view of it.

There is not space here to do any justice to the substantial amount of good Hawthorne criticism that recent years have brought forth. One might mention as instances David Levin's addition of the factor of "spectral evidence" to the interpretation of "Young Goodman Brown," or, on a larger scale, the contributions of Daniel G. Hoffman in *Form and Fable in American Fiction,* or of Richard Chase's *The American Novel and its Tradition,* or R. W. B. Lewis's *The Last Adam.* (Here I must confess that Leslie Fiedler's *Love and Death in American Fiction* is too exciting for me: I have not yet dared to read it.)

"Mythic," Freudian, and Jungian interpretations have appeared in Hawthorne criticism in significant quantity and quality since this book was first published. I am aware of them without wishing to draw upon them more than slightly. Myth and depth-psychology in the hands of skillful critics can add further dimensions and new vitality to a writer's work, but their function in criticism is metaphorical and suggestive; no more than religion, for which they frequently substitute, can they occupy the foreground of interpretation. I have accordingly not altered my text, but rather enlarged it with two new essays, on the tales "My Kinsman, Major Molineux" and

"The Birthmark." Without claiming any finality for my views, I do not wish to second-guess them. Whatever their value, they have been pondered.

RICHARD HARTER FOGLE

*New Orleans*
*September 10, 1964*

# Contents

| | | |
|---|---|---|
| | Preface | *vii* |
| | Preface to the Revised Edition | *ix* |
| I. | The Light and the Dark | 3 |
| II. | "Young Goodman Brown" | 15 |
| III. | "The Minister's Black Veil" | 33 |
| IV. | "Ethan Brand" | 41 |
| V. | "The Maypole of Merry Mount" | 59 |
| VI. | "The Artist of the Beautiful" | 70 |
| VII. | "Rappaccini's Daughter" | 91 |
| VIII. | "My Kinsman, Major Molineux" | 104 |
| IX. | "The Birthmark" | 117 |
| X. | *The Scarlet Letter* | 132 |
| XI. | *The House of the Seven Gables* | 150 |
| XII. | *The Blithedale Romance* | 168 |
| XIII. | *The Marble Faun* | 190 |
| XIV. | Hawthorne's Heaven and Earth | 212 |
| | Index | 235 |

*Hawthorne's Fiction:* THE
LIGHT & THE DARK

# I

## *The Light and the Dark*

HAWTHORNE is a great writer in absolute
terms, and many men have written well about
him. Yet modern critics, led astray by mistaken notions
about realism and by fallacies about inevitable progress,
are still a little condescending. Most general readers,
among them Somerset Maugham, find him naïve and
old-fashioned. Given their perspective, both critics and
readers are honestly reporting what they see; but the
perspective itself is out of focus. A character in Mr. Marquand's recent *Point of No Return* comments sardonical-
ly upon those people who consider *The House of the
Seven Gables* a good story for children. It is a fact that
generations of high-school students have been reared
on the book with no very favorable results. Because of
premature exposure to it, I contracted a dislike for gentle
Phoebe Pyncheon which was surpassed only by my distaste for Lucie Manette in Dickens' *Tale of Two Cities,*
a lady who ranks among the great emetics of English literature. Doubtless most readers remember Hawthorne
from an experience like mine, which also includes mem-
ories of "A Rill from the Town Pump" (interpreted as
a temperance lecture), as it appeared in my eighth-grade
reader.

Hawthorne's writing is misleading in its simplicity,
which is genuine enough but tempts us to overlook what

3

lies beneath. In the end, simplicity is one of his genuine charms—combined with something else. The essence of Hawthorne is, in fact, distilled from the opposing elements of simplicity and complexity. This essence is a clear liquid, with no apparent cloudiness. Hawthorne, together with Henry James, perhaps, is the only American novelist who has been able to see life whole without, in Thackeray's words, "roaring ai, ai, as loud as Prometheus," like Melville, Wolfe, and Faulkner; droning interminably an account of its details, like Dreiser; or falling into a thin, shrill irony, the batlike twittering of souls in Hades, like all the sad young men. Hawthorne's tone is equable, "not harsh nor grating, but with ample power to chasten and subdue." He is a unique and wonderful combination of light and darkness.

The light in Hawthorne is clarity of design. He has a classic balance; his language is exquisitely lucid. He gives one the sense of an invulnerable dignity and centrality; he is impenetrably self-possessed. He holds his characters to the highest standards, for he literally brings them to judgment at the bar of eternity as immortal souls. The "dark" in Hawthorne, that blackness which Herman Melville applauded in him, is his tragic complexity. His clarity is intermingled with subtlety, his statement interfused with symbolism, his affirmation enriched with ambiguity. The whole which results is captivating. In attack he is mild but deadly. His blow is so delicately delivered that a man would have to turn his head in order to realize that he had just lost it. "The Custom House" essay, for example, which rather oddly precedes *The Scarlet Letter*, seems at first sight merely agreeable. Look closer, however, and the effect is devastating. These gently humorous character portraits are murderous, not from malice or

4

heat, but from judgment and icy cold. Hawthorne is not indignant; he is merely certain of his grounds. And his certainty is that of one whose father was called "the sternest man who ever walked a deck."

He is so entirely unsentimental that he does not need, as we sometimes do, to avoid sentimentality. He combines sympathy with a classic aloofness, participation with cool observation. "My father," said Julian Hawthorne, "was two men, one sympathetic and intuitional, the other critical and logical; together they formed a combination which could not be thrown off its feet." Thus Hawthorne's writing has a tone of exquisite gravity, harmonized strangely with a pervasive irony and humor. In the use of irony he is a lighter, more sensitive Fielding, with depths besides which Fielding could not plumb. In the matter of irony Hawthorne's antecedents in the eighteenth-century novel might well be re-examined.

Corresponding to the clarity and the complexity of Hawthorne are his "philosophy" and the crosscurrents which modify its course. For the best understanding one should always attend to the thought of the author. But one grasps that author wholly only by observing his characters, his settings, the patterns of his diction, the trends of his imagery, the concrete mechanics of telling a story. What one has grasped is admittedly not easy to describe, however—therefore the advantage of seizing upon the writer's thought, which can be systematically abstracted.

 The philosophy of Hawthorne is a broadly Christian scheme which contains heaven, earth, and hell. Whether heaven and hell are realities or only subjective states of mind is one of Hawthorne's crucial ambiguities. I do not

5

call him a Christian humanist, as do some excellent critics, for it seems to me that heaven and hell *are* real to him and play too large a part in his fiction to be relegated to the background. In his mixed macrocosm, man is a microcosm also mixed. Man's chief temptation is to forget his limits and complexities, to think himself all good, or to think himself all bad. Either way he falls into spiritual isolation and pride. He needs a proper mixture of the earthly and the ideal—with a touch of the flame to temper it. Thus Aylmer, the scientist-hero of "The Birthmark," violates the covenant of humankind when he tries to eradicate the only blemish of his beautiful wife, a tiny mark on her cheek. He succeeds, but kills her in the process. The birthmark, which is shaped like a hand, is her grip upon earthly existence. She dies to the sound of the laughter of Aminadab, Aylmer's assistant, a kind of earth-fiend. Even the pit has its claims, which must not be slighted. The conclusion epitomizes Hawthorne's thinking: ". . . had Aylmer reached a profounder wisdom, he need not thus have flung away the happiness which would have woven his mortal life of the selfsame texture with the celestial. The momentary circumstance was too strong for him; he failed to look beyond the shadowy scope of time, and living once for all in eternity, to find the perfect future in the present." There is a time for everything, and an eternity. Aylmer should have waited.

But the system does not make the story. The tale of "The Minister's Black Veil" will illustrate the difference between an abstract and a literary meaning. The minister dons the veil as an emblem of secret sin, of which all men are presumably guilty. Elizabeth, his betrothed, implores him to discard it. The minister has found a dreadful truth, while Elizabeth may have discovered a greater

6

—that men are evil *and also* good. The meaning lies not in either but in both. So Hawthorne condemns his strange seekers, his Aylmers, his Ethan Brands, but he makes them noble. His reconciliation is not finally in logic, for he accepts the mystery of existence. His reconciliation is the acceptance itself, realized in balance, structure, and tone.

Hawthorne still suffers from our prejudice against allegory. This prejudice comes partly from a false theory of realism, a legacy of the late nineteenth century, and partly from a misconception of what allegory is. We assume that allegory subordinates everything to a predetermined conclusion: that allegory, in short, is a dishonest counterfeit of literary value. But the great allegories, *The Faerie Queene* and *The Pilgrim's Progress,* possess the literary virtues. And Hawthorne, whose subjects are moral and psychological problems, feels for these problems a passion which transfigures them. All we can ask of a writer is that he treat his material honestly, without unduly simplifying: that he keep faith with his own imagination. T. S. Eliot has said that good religious poetry teaches us not a doctrine but how it feels to believe it; and so it should be with allegory.

Allegory is organic to Hawthorne, an innate quality of his vision. It is his disposition to find spiritual meaning in all things natural and human. This faculty is an inheritance from the Puritans, who saw in everything God's will. To this inheritance was added a gift from nineteenth-century Romanticism, which endowed the natural world with meaning by seeing it as life. In Hawthorne allegory is inseparable from moral complexity and aesthetic design, qualities to be enjoyed in themselves. So,

7

in his "Endicott and the Red Cross" the focus of meaning and the focus of setting are one, and the conclusion takes on an increased value from the subtlety of its preparation. The scene, the village green of seventeenth-century Salem, radiates outward from a center, to return upon it once more. The center is Endicott, the iron Puritan, in whose breastplate, significantly, the scene is mirrored. Endicott is the temporal, active power, the central ethos and intelligence of the story. The Puritan meetinghouse, the spiritual power, is "the central object in the mirrored picture."

On the church porch is nailed the head of a wolf, "a token of the perils of the wilderness." Close by is the whipping-post; at the corners of the meetinghouse stand the pillory and the stocks. Various evildoers are suffering punishment: an Episcopalian, a royalist, a Wanton Gospeller who has given unsanctioned interpretations of Holy Writ, and a woman with her tongue in a cleft stick who has spoken against the elders of the church. There is also "a young woman, with no mean share of beauty," who is condemned to wear upon her breast a scarlet *A*. In the background are armored men, for Endicott is drilling his trainbands.

The Reverend Roger Williams appears—as he might well have done—bearing news of the English crown's intention to send a royal governor to rule the New England colonies. Endicott, in a symbolic gesture of rebellion, rips the cross from the flag of St. George, which flies over the scene.

With a cry of triumph the people gave their sanction to one of the boldest exploits which our history records. And forever honored be the name of Endicott! We look back through the mist of ages, and recognize in the rending of the Red Cross from New England's banner the first omen of that deliverance which our fathers consummated after the bones of the stern Puritans had lain more than a century in the dust.

The story is beautifully compact; it contains an entire era of American history in a single scene and action. The allegorical economy of its dramatis personae is merged with firmly symmetrical composition. The abstract meaning is compressed into one flashing concrete image. The "moral" or summary has considerably more than its surface value, and should be read in the light of the whole story. Before his decisive action Endicott had addressed the crowd, asking rhetorically for what purpose the Puritans fled to the New England wilderness:

"Was it not for liberty to worship God according to our conscience?"

"Call you this liberty of conscience?" interrupted a voice on the steps of the meeting-house.

It was the Wanton Gospeller. A sad and quiet smile flitted across the mild visage of Roger Williams.

Thus the meaning of Endicott's gesture remains, but deeper and richer for the moral complexity of its context. Even so allegorical a figure as Chillingworth, the villain of *The Scarlet Letter*, has his complexities. Hawthorne keeps before our eyes his humanity as well as his evil. So intricate, indeed, are Hawthorne's complications that he has sometimes been accused of indecision. All profound studies of spiritual problems, however, eventually run against a blank wall. Do we know the ultimate des-

9

tiny of James's Isabel Archer? It is a tribute to *The Portrait of a Lady* that the question so much as occurs to us. What do we decide about Conrad's *Lord Jim?* What is the meaning of Jim's one act of cowardice? The whole book tries to tell us, and at the end we are left with the action still unexplained. There is a point where a writer must stop for fear of saying more than his imagination has authorized. The killing of the model is the central action of *The Marble Faun;* yet Donatello kills almost involuntarily, and Miriam, who has incited to murder, is honestly unaware that she has done so. Hawthorne nevertheless holds both to strict account.

This ambiguity in Hawthorne was noticed early but was not fully understood. Contemporary reviews of *The Marble Faun* objected to its vagueness. To friendlier critics Hawthorne's ambiguity was a chiaroscuro effect which deepened the tints of his picture. John Lothrop Motley wrote, "I like those shadowy, weird, fantastic, Hawthornesque shapes flitting through the golden gloom, which is the atmosphere of the book." In his prefaces Hawthorne himself speaks chiefly of this quality of picturesqueness. He says of *The House of the Seven Gables:*

It is a legend prolonging itself, from an epoch now gray in the distance, down into our own broad daylight, and bringing along with it some of its legendary mist, which the reader, according to his pleasure, may either disregard, or allow it to float almost imperceptibly about the characters and events for the sake of a picturesque effect.

This type of ambiguity is a way of introducing the marvelous without offending against probability. It has a deeper purpose, as well—to convey in legend or super-

stition a moral or psychological truth. In the story of the
Pyncheons the whisper of tradition is truer than history;
the legend of Maule's Curse has weighty meaning concealed in it. ". . . ancient superstitions," says Hawthorne,
"after being steeped in human hearts and embodied in
human breath, and passing from lip to ear in manifold
repetition, through a series of generations, become imbued with an effect of homely truth."

Yvor Winters and F. O. Matthiessen have illuminated Hawthorne's ambiguity, which Winters calls "the
formula of alternative possibilities," and Matthiessen
"the device of multiple choice." It is not, however, a device; it is a pervasive quality of mind. It can be an
evasion, and it is sometimes no more than a mannerism.
But as a whole it embodies Hawthorne's deepest insights.
It oulines the pure form of truth by dissolving irrelevan-
cies; this is its positive function. Negatively, it marks the
limit of eyeshot, beyond which is shadow. Thus Hawthorne's effects of light—his shadows, his mirror images,
his masquerades—all examine the relationships of appearance and reality. Hawthorne's ambiguity involves
both light and darkness. As light it is the means of seeing
through opacities; as darkness it is the difficulty of seeing.

Hawthorne's simplest ambiguity is a playful mystification. In retelling the Greek myths in *A Wonder-Book*
and *Tanglewood Tales* he uses ambiguity to introduce
the Olympian gods. Mortals continually have glimpses
of the supernatural. In "The Miraculous Pitcher" old
Baucis and Philemon entertain Jove and Mercury, who
are disguised as casual wayfarers. The old couple see
miracles without being able to believe their eyes, and
Hawthorne also pretends to be skeptical. Thus Mercury's
caduceus is ostensibly an optical illusion:

Two snakes, carved in the wood, were represented as twining themselves about the staff, and were so very skilfully executed that old Philemon (whose eyes, you know, were getting rather dim) almost thought them alive, and that he could see them wriggling and twisting.

(This same staff is used more seriously in "Young Goodman Brown" and *The Blithedale Romance*, in both of which it indicates the presence of evil.) This ambiguity is proper to the children's tale; as with fairy stories, what is required is not real belief, but a temporary suspension of disbelief. Yet even here there is a hint of truth before eyes too blind to see it.

The issues are more serious in such legends of New England as "The Gray Champion" and the "Legends of the Province House" in the volume of *Twice-Told Tales*. In these stories the ambiguity underlines the significance by dissolving irrelevant actuality in the mists of the past and leaving only an ideal history. Ambiguity invests the events with the rich pathos and patina of time and counterpoints unreality against truth. In "The Gray Champion" the hero's background is shadowed, the better to project his image in the foreground. In "Howe's Masquerade" disguise reveals identity; the procession of royal governors is a masquerade, but there is nothing false about its meaning. The ambiguity of the "Legends" is a vision of the Past in the light of the Present, a picture in a frame of distance.

Hawthorne uses ambiguity structurally to create suspense and retard conclusions, especially in tales where the primary emphasis would otherwise be too clear. "The Celestial Railroad," an ironic nineteenth-century *Pilgrim's Progress*, is an example of this usage. Hawthorne's railroad is scheduled to the Celestial City, but its real destination is Hell. By disguising the way to Perdition as the road to Heaven, he takes the reader into his confidence by a sustained ironic reversal of values and curbs impatience for the end by supplying attractions on the way. "The Celestial Railroad," however, is closer to abstract allegory than Hawthorne generally gets. More fundamental is the tragic ambiguity which threatens the bases of accepted values, as in "Young Goodman Brown," where the final interpretation is in genuine doubt. Hawthorne judges relentlessly, yet with sympathy, and his ambiguity always leaves room for a different verdict. He preserves the sanctity and independence of his characters by allowing them at bottom an inviolable individuality.

In their recently published *Theory of Literature*, Rene Wellek and Austin Warren define the symbol as "an object which refers to another object but which demands attention also in its own right, as a presentation." The symbol must be interesting in itself, not merely as it points to something else. This crucial requirement, which divides *mere* allegory from literature, Hawthorne fulfills. The minister's black veil is truly a veil, as well as an emblem of secret sin. The brook of *The Scarlet Letter* has water in it, though it symbolizes life and time. The fountain in Rappaccini's garden is an object of art in addition to being an image of eternity. Hawthorne's symbols have the clarity of allegory, with the complexity and density of life. They are rarely obscure, but they will abide the test of long use without wearing out. Since they are generally accompanied by an explanation, it is natural to pass by them quickly—too quickly.

The rosebush before the prison in Chapter I of *The*

13

*Scarlet Letter* is an instance of this misleading simplicity. It stands, says Hawthorne, "in token that the deep heart of nature can pity and forgive." The rose is pitying nature, as the prison is pitiless man. The rose is also, however, Hester Prynne, a red rose against the gray Puritan background; and therefore it is the scarlet letter, the natural passion which the prison exists to quell. Beside the fortress-like prison the rose seems pitiably frail, but it is strong with the power of natural vitality.

Hawthorne's symbols are broadly traditional, drawn from the main stream of Western thought. In his pages are the red cavern of the heart and the gray cavern of isolation; the wild forest and the winding path of error (from Spenser); the fountain and the sea of eternity, and the river of time; the Garden of Eden, with Adam and Eve and the serpent; the flames of hell, strangely mingled with the forge fire of Vulcan's smithy, and the bright blaze of the hearth; the devil's stigmata, and the sunlight of holiness. Created as they are of old materials, these symbols are yet fresh from Hawthorne's imagination. He invests them with a new vitality and suggestiveness.

## II

# *"Young Goodman Brown"*

"YOUNG GOODMAN BROWN" is generally felt to be one of Hawthorne's more difficult tales, from the ambiguity of the conclusions which may be drawn from it. Its hero, a naïve young man who accepts both society in general and his fellow men as individuals at their own valuation, is in one terrible night confronted with the vision of human evil, and is ever afterwards "a stern, a sad, a darkly meditative, a distrustful, if not a desperate man . . ." whose "dying hour was gloom." So far we are clear enough, but there are confusing factors. In the first place, are the events of the night merely subjective, a dream, or do they actually occur? Again, at the crucial point in his ordeal Goodman Brown summons the strength to cry to his wife Faith, "look up to heaven, and resist the evil one." It would appear from this that he had successfully resisted the supreme temptation— but evidently he is not therefore saved. Henceforth, "on the Sabbath day, when the congregation were singing a holy psalm, he could not listen because an anthem of sin rushed loudly upon his ear and drowned all the blessed strain." On the other hand he is not wholly lost, for he is only at intervals estranged from "the bosom of Faith." Has Hawthorne failed to control the implications of his allegory?

I should say rather that these ambiguities of meaning are intentional, an integral part of his purpose. He does not wish to propose flatly that man is primarily evil; rather he has a gnawing fear that this might indeed be true. "Come, devil; for to thee is this world given," exclaims Goodman Brown at the height of his agony. But he finds strength to resist the devil, and in the ambiguous conclusion he does not entirely reject his former faith. His trial, then, comes not from the certainty but from the dread of Evil. Hawthorne poses the dangerous question of the relations of Good and Evil in man but withholds his answer. Nor does he permit himself to determine whether the events of the night of trial are real or the mere figment of a dream.

These ambiguities he conveys and fortifies by what Yvor Winters has called "the formula of alternative possibilities," and F. O. Matthiessen "the device of multiple choice," in which are suggested two or more interpretations of a single action or event. Perhaps the most striking instance of the use of this device in "Young Goodman Brown" is the final word on the reality of the hero's night experience:

Had Goodman Brown fallen asleep in the forest and only dreamed a wild dream of a witch-meeting?

*Be it so if you will;*[1] but alas! it was a dream of evil omen for young Goodman Brown.

This device of multiple choice, or ambiguity, is the very essence of Hawthorne's tale. Nowhere does he permit us a simple meaning, a merely single interpretation. At the outset young Goodman Brown leaves the arms of his wife Faith and the safe limits of Salem to keep a

[1] These and all subsequent italics are mine.

mysterious appointment in the forest. Soon he encounters his guide, a man "in grave and decent attire," commonplace enough save for an indefinable air of acquaintanceship with the great world. ". . . the only thing about him that could be fixed upon as remarkable was his staff, which bore the likeness of a great black snake, so curiously wrought that it might almost be seen to twist and wriggle itself like a living serpent. *This, of course, must have been an ocular deception, assisted by the uncertain light.*"

This man is, of course, the Devil, who seeks to lure the still-reluctant goodman to a witch-meeting. In the process he progressively undermines the young man's faith in the institutions and the men whom he has heretofore revered. First Goody Cloyse, "a very pious and exemplary dame, who had taught him his catechism in youth, and was still his moral and spiritual adviser," is shown to have more than casual acquaintance with the Devil—to be, in fact, a witch. Goodman Brown is shaken, but still minded to turn back and save himself. He is then faced with a still harder test. Just as he is about to return home, filled with self-applause, he hears the tramp of horses along the road:

On came the hoof tramps and the voices of the riders, two grave old voices, conversing soberly as they drew near. These mingled sounds appeared to pass along the road, within a few yards of the young man's hiding-place; *but, owing doubtless to the depth of the gloom at that particular spot, neither the travellers nor their steeds were visible. Though their figures brushed the small boughs by the wayside, it could not be seen that they intercepted, even for a moment, the faint gleam from the strip of bright sky athwart which they must have passed.* It vexed him the more, because he could have sworn, *were such a thing possible,* that he recognized the voices of the minister and Deacon Gookin, jogging along quietly, as they were wont to do, when bound to some ordination or ecclesiastical council.

The conversation of the minister and the deacon makes it only too clear that they also are in league with the Devil. Yet Goodman Brown, although now even more deeply dismayed, still resolves to stand firm, heartened by the blue arch of the sky and the stars brightening in it. At that moment a cloud, "though no wind was stirring," hides the stars, and he hears a confused babble of voices. *"Once the listener fancied that he could distinguish* the accents of townspeople of his own. . . . The next moment, so indistinct were the sounds, *he doubted whether he had heard aught* but the murmur of the old forest, whispering without a wind." But to his horror he believes that he hears the voice of his wife Faith, uttering only weak and insincere objections as she is borne through the air to the witch-meeting.

Now comes an event which at first would appear to break the chain of ambiguities, for Goodman Brown's suspicions seem concretely verified. A pink ribbon, which he remembers having seen in his wife's hair, comes fluttering down into his grasp. This ribbon, apparently a solid object like the fatal handkerchief in *Othello,* seems out of keeping with the atmosphere of doubt which has enveloped the preceding incidents. Two considerations, however, make it possible to account for its appearance. One is that if Goodman Brown is dreaming the ribbon may be taken as part and parcel of his dream. It is to be noted that this pink ribbon appears in his wife's hair once more as she meets him on his return to Salem the next morning. The other is that for the moment the ribbon vanishes from the story, melting into its shadowy background. Its impact is merely temporary.

Be it as you will, as Hawthorne would say. At any rate, the effect on Goodman Brown is instantaneous and devastating. Casting aside all further scruples, he rages through the wild forest to the meeting of witches, for the time at least fully accepting the domination of Evil. He soon comes upon a large gathering, alternately shadowy and clear in the flickering red light of four blazing pines above a central rock.

Among them, *quivering to and fro between gloom and splendor,* appeared faces that would be seen next day at the council board of the province, and others which, Sabbath after Sabbath, looked devoutly heavenward, and benignantly over the crowded pews, from the holiest pulpits in the land. *Some affirm that* the lady of the governor was there. . . . *Either the sudden gleams of light flashing over the obscure field bedazzled Goodman Brown, or he recognized* a score of the church members of Salem village famous for their especial sanctity.

Before this company steps out a presiding figure who bears "with reverence be it spoken . . . *no slight similitude,* both in garb and manner, to some grave divine of the New England churches," and calls forth the "converts." At the word young Goodman Brown comes forward. *"He could have well-nigh sworn that* the shape of his own dead father beckoned him to advance, looking downward from a smoke wreath, while a woman, with dim features of despair, threw out her hand to warn him back. *Was it his mother?"* But he is quickly seized and led to the rock,

19

along with a veiled woman whom he dimly discerns to be his wife Faith. The two are welcomed by the dark and ambiguous leader into the fraternity of Evil, and the final, irretrievable step is prepared.

A basin was hollowed, naturally, in the rock. *Did it contain water, reddened by the lurid light? or perchance, a liquid flame?* Herein did the shape of evil dip his hand and prepare to lay the mark of baptism upon their foreheads, that they might be partakers of the mystery of sin, more conscious of the secret guilt of others, both in deed and thought, than they could now be of their own. The husband cast one look at his pale wife, and Faith at him. What polluted wretches would the next glance show them to each other, shuddering alike at what they disclosed and what they saw! "Faith! Faith!" cried the husband, "look up to heaven, and resist the wicked one."

*Whether Faith obeyed he knew not.*

Hawthorne then concludes with the central ambiguity, which we have already noticed, whether the events of the night were actual or a dream. The uses of this device, if so it may be called, are multiple in consonance with its nature. Primarily it offers opportunity for freedom and richness of suggestion. By it Hawthorne is able to suggest something of the density and incalculability of life, the difficulties which clog the interpretation of even the simplest incidents, the impossibility of achieving a single and certain insight into the actions and motives of others. This ambiguity adds depth and tone to Hawthorne's thin and delicate fabric. It covers the bareness of allegory, imparting to its one-to-one equivalence of object and idea a wider range of allusiveness, a hint of rich meaning still untapped. By means of it the thesis of "Young Goodman Brown" is made to inhere firmly in the situation, and the reader himself must extract it to interpret. Hawthorne refuses to limit himself to a single and doctrinaire conclusion, proceeding instead by indirection. Further, this ambiguity permits the author to make free of the two opposed worlds of actuality and imagination without incongruity or the need to commit himself entirely to either. While avoiding a frontal attack upon the reader's feeling for everyday verisimilitude, it affords the author license of fancy. It allows him to draw upon sources of legend and superstition which still strike a responsive chord in us and possess something of the validity of universal symbols. Hawthorne's own definition of romance may very aptly be applied to his use of ambiguity: it gives him scope "so [to] manage his atmospherical medium as to bring out or mellow the lights and deepen and enrich the shadows of the picture."

Above all, the separate instances of the "multiple choice device" organically unite to reproduce in the reader's mind the feel of the central ambiguity of theme—the horror of the hero's doubt. Goodman Brown, a simple and pious nature, is wrecked as a result of the disappearance of the fixed poles of his belief. His orderly cosmos dissolves into chaos as church and state, the twin pillars of his society, are hinted to be rotten, with their foundations undermined. The yearning for certainty is basic to his spirit—and he is left without even the comfort of a firm reliance in the Devil. His better qualities avail him in his desperation little more than the inner evil which prompted him to court temptation, for they prevent him from seeking the only remaining refuge—the confraternity of Sin. Henceforth he is fated to battle with

21

shadows, to struggle with limed feet toward a redemption which must forever elude him, since he has lost the vision of Good while rejecting the opportunity to embrace Evil fully. Individual instances of ambiguity, then, merge and coalesce in the theme itself to produce an all-pervading atmosphere of uneasiness and anguished doubt.

Ambiguity alone, however, is not a satisfactory aesthetic principle. Flexibility, suggestiveness, allusiveness, variety—all these are without meaning if there is no pattern from which to vary, no center from which to radiate. And, indeed, ambiguity of itself will not adequately account for the individual phenomenon of "Young Goodman Brown." The deliberate haziness and multiple implications of its meaning are counterbalanced by the firm clarity of its technique, in structure and in style.

This clarity is embodied in the lucid simplicity of the basic action; in the skillful foreshadowing by which the plot is bound together; in the balance of episode and scene; in the continuous use of contrast; in the firmness and selectivity of Hawthorne's pictorial composition; in the carefully arranged climactic order of incident and tone; in the detachment and irony of Hawthorne's attitude; and finally in the purity, the grave formality, and the rhetorical balance of the style. His amalgamation of these elements reveals consummate artistic economy in fitting the means to the attempted ends.

The general framework of the story has a large simplicity. At sunset Goodman Brown leaves his wife Faith and the safe confines of Salem, spends the night in the forest, and at dawn returns a changed man. Within this simple pattern, plot and allegory unfold symmetrically and simultaneously. The movement of "Young Goodman Brown" is the single revolution of a wheel, which

turns full circle upon itself. Apart from this basic structure, the action is also given form by the device of foreshadowing, through which the entire development of the
plot is made implicit in the opening paragraph. Faith is
troubled by her husband's expedition and begs him to put
it off till sunrise. " 'A lone woman is troubled with such
dreams and such thoughts that she's afeared of herself
sometimes,' " says she, hinting the sequel of her own
baptism in sin. " 'My love and my Faith,' replied young
Goodman Brown, 'of all nights in the year, this one night
must I tarry away from thee. My journey . . . forth and
back again, must needs be done 'twixt now and sunrise.' "
They part, but looking back Brown sees "the head of
Faith still peeping after him with a melancholy air, in
spite of her pink ribbons."

"Poor little Faith!" thought he, for his heart smote him.
"What a wretch am I to leave her on such an errand! She
talks of dreams, too. Methought as she spoke there was
trouble in her face, as if a dream had warned her what work
is to be done to-night. But no, no; 'twould kill her to think
of it. Well, she's a blessed angel on earth; and after this one
night I'll cling to her skirts and follow her to heaven."

This speech is in several respects clumsy, obvious,
and melodramatic; but beneath the surface is a deeper
layer. The pervasive ambiguity of the story is foreshadowed in the subtle emphasizing of the dream motif,
which paves the way for the ultimate uncertainty whether
the incidents of the night are dream or reality; and in his
simple-minded aspirations to " 'cling to her skirts and
follow her to heaven' " Goodman Brown is laying an
ironic foundation for his later horror of doubt. A broader

irony is apparent, in the light of later events, in the general emphasis upon Faith's angelic goodness.

Hawthorne's seemingly casual references to Faith's pink ribbons, which are mentioned three times in the opening paragraphs, are likewise far from artless. These ribbons, as we have seen, are an important factor in the plot, and as an emblem of heavenly faith their color gradually deepens into the liquid flame or blood of the baptism into sin.

Another instance of Hawthorne's careful workmanship is his architectural balance of episodes or scenes. The encounter with Goody Cloyse, the female hypocrite and sinner, is set off against the conversation of the minister and Deacon Gookin immediately afterward. The exact correspondence of the two episodes is brought into high relief by two balancing speeches. Goody Cloyse has lost her broomstick, and must perforce walk to the witch-meeting—a sacrifice she is willing to make since " 'they tell me there is a nice young man to be taken into communion to-night.' " A few minutes later Deacon Gookin remarks that " 'there is a goodly young woman to be taken into communion.' " A still more significant example of this balance is contained in the full swing of the wheel—in the departure at sunset and the return at sunrise. At the beginning of the story Brown takes leave of "Faith with the pink ribbons," turns the corner by the meeting-house, and leaves the town; in the conclusion

. . . Young Goodman Brown came slowly into the street of Salem village, staring around him like a bewildered man. The good old minister was taking a walk along the grave-yard to get an appetite for breakfast and meditate his sermon, and bestowed a blessing, as he passed, on Goodman

Brown. He shrank from the venerable saint as if to avoid
an anathema. Old Deacon Gookin was at domestic worship,
and the holy words of his prayer were heard through the
open window. "What God doth the wizard pray to?" quoth
Goodman Brown. Goody Cloyse, that excellent old Christian, stood in the early sunshine at her own lattice, catechiz-
ing a little girl who had brought her a pint of morning's
milk. Goodman Brown snatched the child away as from the
grasp of the fiend himself. Turning the corner by the meeting-house, he spied the head of Faith, with the pink ribbons,
gazing anxiously forth, and bursting into such joy at the
sight of him that she skipped along the street and almost
kissed her husband before the whole village. But Goodman
Brown looked sternly and sadly into her face, and passed
on without a greeting.

The exact parallel between the earlier and the later situations serves to dramatize intensely the change which the
real or fancied happenings of the night have brought
about in Goodman Brown.

Contrast, a form of balance, is still more prominent
in "Young Goodman Brown" than the analogy of scene
and episode which I have mentioned. The broad antitheses of day and night, town and forest, both of which sig-
nify in general a sharp dualism of Good and Evil, are
supplemented by a color contrast of red and black at the
witch meeting, by the swift transition of the forest scene
from leaping flame to damp and chill, and by the consistent cleavage between outward decorum and inner corruption in the characters.

The symbols of Day and Night, of Town and Forest,
are almost indistinguishable in meaning. Goodman Brown
leaves the limits of Salem at dusk and re-enters them at

sunrise; he spends the intervening night in the forest. Day and the Town are clearly emblematic of Good, of the seemly outward appearance of human convention and society. They stand for the safety of an unquestioning and unspeculative faith. Oddly enough, in the daylight of the Salem streets Goodman Brown is too simple and straightforward to be interesting and is somewhat distasteful in his boundless reverence for such unspectacular worthies as the minister, the deacon, and Goody Cloyse. Night and the Forest, symbols of doubt and wandering, are the domains of the Evil One, where the dark subterranean forces of the human spirit riot unchecked. By the dramatic necessities of the plot Brown is a larger figure in the Forest of Evil and at the witch-meeting than he is within the safe bounds of the town.

The contrast of the red of fire and blood and the black of night and forest at the witch-meeting has a different import. As the flames rise and fall, the faces of the worshipers of Evil are alternately seen in clear outline and in deep shadow, and all the details of the scene are at one moment revealed, the next obscured. It seems, then, that red represents Sin or Evil, plain and unequivocal; black represents that doubt of the reality of either Evil or Good which tortures Goodman Brown. A further contrast follows in the swift transformation of scene, when young Goodman Brown finds himself "amid calm night and solitude. . . . He staggered against the rock, and felt it chill and damp; while a hanging twig, that had been all on fire, besprinkled his cheek with the coldest dew."

Most pervasive of the contrasts in "Young Goodman Brown" is the consistent discrepancy between appearance and reality, which helps to produce the heavy atmosphere of doubt and shadow. The church is represented by the highly respectable figures of Goody Cloyse, the minister, and Deacon Gookin, who in the forest are witch and wizards. The devil appears in the guise of Brown's grandfather. As the goodman approaches the meeting, his ears are greeted by "the swell of what seemed a hymn, rolling solemnly from a distance with the weight of many voices. He knew the tune; it was a familiar one in the choir of the village meeting-house." The Communion of Sin is, in fact, the faithful counterpart of a grave and pious ceremony at a Puritan meetinghouse. "At one extremity of an open space, hemmed in by the dark wall of the forest, arose a rock, bearing some rude, natural resemblance either to an altar or a pulpit, and surrounded by four blazing pines, their tops aflame, their stems untouched, like candles at an evening meeting." The worshipers are "a numerous congregation," Satan resembles some grave divine, and the initiation into sin takes the form of a baptism.

Along with this steady use of contrast in the Sabbath scene should be noticed the firmly composed pictorial quality. The rock, the center of the picture, is lighted by blazing pines. The chief actors are, as it were, spotlighted in turn as they advance to the rock, while the congregation is generalized in the dimmer light at the outer edges. The whole composition is simple and definite, in contrast to the ambiguity occasioned by the rise and fall of the flame, in which the mass of the worshipers alternately shines forth and disappears in shadow.

The clarity and simple structural solidity of "Young Goodman Brown" evinces itself in its tight dramatic framework. Within the basic form of the turning wheel the story further divides into four separate scenes, the first and last of which, are, of course, the balancing departure from and return to Salem. The night in the forest falls naturally into two parts: the temptation by the Devil and the witch-meeting. These two scenes, particularly the first, make full and careful use of the dramatic devices of suspense and climactic arrangement, and Hawthorne manipulates his materials to divide them as sharply as by a dropped curtain.

The temptation at first has the stylized and abstract delicacy of Restoration comedy or of the formalized seductions of Molière's *Don Juan*. The simple goodman, half-eager and half-reluctant, is wholly at the mercy of Satan, who leads him step by step to the inevitable end. The lightly ironic tone of the earlier part of this scene is reinforced by the inherent irony of the situation, which elicits a double meaning at every turn.

"Come, Goodman Brown," cried his fellow-traveller, "this is a dull pace for the beginning of a journey. Take my staff, if you are so soon weary."

"Friend," said the other, exchanging his slow pace for a full stop, "having kept covenant by meeting thee here, it is my purpose now to return whence I came. I have scruples touching the matter thou wot'st of."

"Sayest thou so?" replied he of the serpent, smiling apart. "Let us walk on, nevertheless, reasoning as we go; and if I convince thee not thou shalt turn back. We are but a little way in the forest yet."

Then commences a skillful and relentless attack on all the values which Goodman Brown has lived by. His reverence for his Puritan ancestors, "a people of prayer, and good works to boot," is speedily turned against him as the Devil claims them for tried and dear companions. Next comes the encounter with Goody Cloyse, who taught the young man his catechism. Brown is sorely cast down, but at length sturdily concludes, "What if a wretched old woman do choose to go to the devil when I thought she was going to heaven: is that any reason why I should quit my dear Faith and go after her?" But no sooner has he rallied from this blow than he is hit by another, still more shrewdly placed: he hears the voices of the minister and Deacon Gookin, and from their conversation gathers that they are bound for the meeting and are eagerly anticipating it. This is almost the final thrust, but still Brown holds out. " 'With heaven above, and Faith below, I will yet stand firm against the devil!' " he cries, only to be utterly overthrown by the sound of his wife's voice and the crushing evidence of the pink ribbon.

The style has gradually deepened and intensified with the carefully graduated intensity of the action, and now Hawthorne lets it out full. Nature is made at once to sympathize with and to mock the anguished chaos in Goodman Brown; in his rage the hero is both united with and opposed to the forest and the wind. The symphony of sound, which began with the confused babble of voices in the sky as Faith and her witch-attendants swept overhead, rises to a wild crescendo.

And, maddened with despair, so that he laughed loud and long, did Goodman Brown grasp his staff and set forth again, at such a rate that he seemed to fly along the forest path rather than to walk or run. The road grew wilder and drearier and more faintly traced, and vanished at length, leaving him in the heart of the dark wilderness, still rushing onward with the instinct that guides mortal man to evil.

29

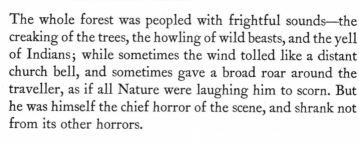

The whole forest was peopled with frightful sounds—the creaking of the trees, the howling of wild beasts, and the yell of Indians; while sometimes the wind tolled like a distant church bell, and sometimes gave a broad roar around the traveller, as if all Nature were laughing him to scorn. But he was himself the chief horror of the scene, and shrank not from its other horrors.

After ascending to this climax Hawthorne disengages himself and separates his scenes by the simple expedient of shifting his view from the hero to the hero's surroundings. Goodman Brown is a mere onlooker at the witch-meeting until the moment comes for him to step forward for his baptism into sin. Up to that point Satan usurps the stage. The eye is first directed to the central rock-altar, then to the four blazing pines which light it. Next there is the impression of a large assembly, vaguely seen in the fitful firelight. Finally the figure of Satan appears at the base of the rock, framed in an arch of flame. Only when he is summoned are we once more fully aware of Goodman Brown, as he stands at the altar by his wife. A moment later comes the second climax, when Brown calls upon his wife to " 'look up to heaven, and resist the wicked one' "—cut off abruptly by anticlimax as the meeting vanishes in a roaring wind, and Brown leaning against the rock finds it chill and damp to his touch.

The satisfaction one feels in the clean line of the story's structure is enhanced by Hawthorne's steady detachment from his materials, an attitude which deepens the impression of classic balance, which in turn stands against the painful ambiguity of the theme. Even the full tone of the most intense scenes, as the one in which Goodman Brown rushes through the forest, is tempered by restraint. The participant is overweighted by the calm, impartial (though not unfeeling) spectator; Hawthorne does not permit himself to become identified with his hero. He displays young Goodman Brown not in and for the hero himself, but always in relation to the whole situation and set of circumstances. This detachment of attitude is plainest in the almost continuous irony, unemphatic but nonetheless relentless: an irony organically related to the ever-present ambiguities of the situation, but most evident in sustained tone. Thus, after recording Goodman Brown's aspiration to " 'cling to Faith's skirts and follow her to heaven,' " the author adds with deadly calm, "With this excellent resolve for the future, Goodman Brown felt himself justified in making more haste on his present evil purpose."

This detachment is implicit in the quiet, the abstractness, and the gravity of Hawthorne's style, which is everywhere formal and exactly, though subtly, cadenced. It throws a light and idealizing veil over the action and maintains an aesthetic distance, while hinting at the ugliness it covers. The difference between the saying and the thing said provides dramatic tension. Note, for example, the grave decorum, the eighteenth-century stateliness, and the perverted courtliness of Satan's welcome to young Brown and Faith:

"This night it shall be granted you to know their secret deeds: how hoary-bearded elders of the church have whispered wanton words to the young maids of their households; how many a woman, eager for widows' weeds, has given her husband a drink at bedtime and let him sleep his last sleep in her bosom; how beardless youths have made haste to inherit their fathers' wealth; and how fair damsels—

31

blush not, sweet ones—have dug little graves in the garden, and bidden me, the sole guest, to an infant's funeral."

The steady procession of measured, ceremonious generalizations—"hoary-bearded elders," "wanton words," "beardless youths," "fair damsels," and so on—is in radical contrast to the implication of the meaning; and the grisly archness of "blush not, sweet ones" is suggestive in its incongruity.

In "Young Goodman Brown," then, Hawthorne has achieved that reconciliation of opposites which Coleridge considered the highest art. The combination of clarity of technique—embodied in simplicity and balance of structure, in firm pictorial composition, in contrast and climactic arrangement, in irony and detachment—with ambiguity of meaning, as signalized by the "device of multiple choice," in its interrelationships produces the story's characteristic effect. By means of these two elements Hawthorne reconciles oneness of action with multiplicity of suggestion and enriches the bareness of systematic allegory. Contrarily, by them he avoids lapsing into mere speculation without substance or form. The phantasmagoric light and shadow of the rising and falling fire, which obscures and softens the clear, hard outline of the witch-meeting, is an image which will stand for the essential effect of the story itself, an effect compacted of ambiguity and clarity harmoniously interfused.

# III

## *"The Minister's Black Veil"*

HAWTHORNE's characteristic fusion of surface simplicity and underlying complexity is perhaps nowhere more clearly evident than in "The Minister's Black Veil," a brief, highly typical, and thoroughly successful story. It is subtitled "A Parable," and the outer meaning of the parable is abundantly clear. An apparently blameless minister inexplicably dons a black veil and wears it throughout his lifetime, despite many well-meant pleas to cast it off. On his deathbed he reveals its secret and its justification:

"What, but the mystery which it obscurely typifies, has made this piece of crape so awful? When the friend shows his inmost heart to his friend; the lover to his best beloved; when man does not vainly shrink from the eye of his Creator, loathsomely treasuring up the secret of his sin; then deem me a monster, for the symbol beneath which I have lived, and die! I look around me, and, lo! on every visage a Black Veil!"

The moral is impressive; but as a proposition it is not difficult to grasp, however it may wind and reverberate within the deeps of the imagination. The veil as the visible symbol of secret sin was suggested by Hawthorne's reading in New England history and legend. The veil's solid actuality has the effect of isolating the minister from human society, which unhappy result presumably differs only in degree from the self-isolation of every living soul. The minister is Everyman, bearing his lonely fate in order to demonstrate a tragic truth.

The moral is explicit and orthodox. The explicit statement, however, leads to more than a single possibility. The self-imposed martyrdom of Father Hooper must correspond with some deep necessity of his nature. He who isolates himself in the outward fact must already have performed the deed in spirit. The act of donning the veil has in it something of caprice; it is entirely out of proportion to any obvious necessity or benefit. By it the minister forfeits the affection of his congregation, the chance of human love and marriage, and the sympathy of society in general—and to what end? No note of triumph sounds for him. With remorseless consistency, Hawthorne pursues him even into the grave. "Still veiled, they laid him in his coffin, and a veiled corpse they bore him to the grave. The grass of many years has sprung up and withered on that grave, the burial-stone is moss-grown, and good Mr. Hooper's face is dust; but awful still is the thought that it mouldered beneath the Black Veil!"

One may feel that the veil is less representative of mankind than of the eccentricity of the minister himself, who severs himself from men either through perverse pride or through some other obscure and tragic compulsion. His preoccupation with sin has blunted his perceptions of the normal and the good, which lie as ready to his hand as evil. In rejecting the love of his betrothed, Elizabeth, he casts away a gift of inestimable value in order to satisfy a wild obsession.

If we continue with this reading of the story, we shall take Elizabeth to exemplify the normal and well-ordered human being, as Mr. Hooper represents the abnormal, who has lost the power of seeing life steadily and whole. The "calm energy" of her character, her "direct simplicity," contrasts with the "gentle, but unconquerable obstinacy" of the minister, whom her good counsel fails to persuade, and with his infatuated love of mystification. Hawthorne inherited the psychology, but not the theology nor the morality of his Puritan ancestors; and Elizabeth is more likely to represent his ideal than is the gloomy and sin-crazed Hooper.

Which, then, of these two interpretations shall we accept? Both, I believe—they are both in the story. Either presents its difficulties. If we take "The Minister's Black Veil" at its face value as a homily on secret sin, we are confronted with the apparent disproportion between the act and its causes. The minister himself is to outward gaze the gentlest and least sinful of men; and we have no vivid sense of that presence of Evil which would necessitate so heroic an object lesson. But if we wholly accede to the second interpretation, which makes the steady view of life, the *aurea mediocritas*, the highest good, then the tone and emphasis of the story remain to be explained. It is too deeply gloomy and intense to harmonize fully with such a moral, which should demand a certain dry sparkle and lightness.

This ambivalence of meaning is realized in ambiguity, which occurs with unusual frequency in "The Minister's Black Veil." Here its most marked effect is to maintain a balance between subjective and objective in the portrait of the minister, to invite us inside his character while excluding us from any final certainty about it, and, of course, to preserve the objectivity of the narrator, who simultaneously offers and reserves his judgment. Thus, for example, we do not quite know what Mr. Hooper saw through the veil, "which entirely concealed his features, except the mouth and chin, but *probably* did not intercept his sight, further than to give a darkened aspect to all living and inanimate things." The word "probably" bars us from certainty on the point. Again, as the minister preaches for the first time from beneath the veil, it "lay heavily on his uplifted countenance. Did he seek to hide it from the dread Being whom he was addressing?" Hawthorne proposes the question, but does not answer it.

Pressed by Elizabeth to expound the meaning of the veil, Mr. Hooper will reply only darkly. " 'If it be a sign of mourning,' " says he, " 'I, perhaps, like most other mortals, have sorrows dark enough to be typified by a black veil.' " When she further relates the scandalous whispers in the village that he hides his face from consciousness of secret sin, he will not deny the imputation. " 'If I hide my face for sorrow, there is cause enough,' " he merely replies; " 'and if I cover it for secret sin, what mortal might not do the same?' " Hawthorne holds out the suggestion that the veil is a penance for an actual and serious crime, while at the same time permitting no real grounds for it. The vulgar interpret the meaning vulgarly, the complacent complacently, and men of good will regretfully. The calm good sense of Elizabeth forces her to regard the veil as the emblem of a tragic but unbased obsession. She believes at first that " 'there is nothing terrible in this piece of crape' " but at length yields to its influence, not from a dread of the veil itself, but of what the veil tells her of her lover's state of mind.

The mystery of the veil is hidden to the end among these artfully contrived ambiguities. As Elizabeth leaves him, "Mr. Hooper smiled to think that only a material emblem had separated him from happiness, though the horrors, which it shadowed forth, must be drawn darkly between the fondest of lovers." It is confusing to have the symbol detached from its meaning in this fashion; and the passage calls up another consideration. If the veil alone has separated the minister from happiness, what are we to do with "the horrors, which it shadowed forth?" Surely it is they which shut him off from earthly good. The effect is at once to assert and to cast doubt on the reality of what the veil portrays but also hides. And the smile itself, shining dimly from beneath the black cloth, emphasizes in its self-irony the ambiguity of the minister's character.

The veil has varying effects on different minds and different levels of society. To those "who claimed a superiority to popular prejudice," it is merely "an eccentric whim." In the multitude it occasions either impertinence or superstitious dread, reactions equally grievous to its unhappy wearer. It is whispered that the veil is the obscure intimation of a horrible crime; and there are hints of supernatural forces:

Thus, from beneath the black veil, there rolled a cloud into the sunshine, *an ambiguity of sin or sorrow,* which enveloped the poor minister, so that love or sympathy could never reach him. *It was said* that ghost and fiend consorted with him there. With self-shudderings and outward terrors, he walked continually in its shadow, groping darkly within his own soul, or gazing through a medium that saddened the whole world. Even the lawless wind, *it was believed,* respected his dreadful secret, and never blew aside the veil. But still good Mr. Hooper sadly smiled at the pale visages of the worldly throng as he passed by.

In one respect, however, the veil makes Mr. Hooper a more efficient clergyman, for it allows him to "sympathize with all dark affections." His words are imbued with its gloomy power, and he can bring sinners to the light denied to him. Yet here as well the effects of the veil are ambiguous. His converts regard the minister with dread, not with love or joy, even though they owe their redemption to him. "Dying sinners cried aloud for Mr. Hooper, and would not yield their breath till he appeared; though ever, as he stooped to whisper consolation, they shuddered at the veiled face so near their own." Hawthorne summarizes the twofold influence of the veil in a climactic ambiguity which embodies its dualism in a series of antitheses: "In this manner Mr. Hooper spent a long life, irreproachable in outward act, yet shrouded in dismal suspicions; kind and loving, though unloved, and dimly feared; a man apart from men, shunned in their health and joy, but ever summoned to their aid in mortal anguish."

This dubiety persists in the final scene at the deathbed, despite the explicit pronouncement with which the scene ends. As the minister lies dying, the veil still rests upon his face, stirred slightly by his faint breath. "All through life that piece of crape had hung between him and the world; it had separated him from cheerful brotherhood and woman's love, and kept him in that saddest of all prisons, his own heart; and still it lay upon his face, as if to deepen the gloom of his darksome chamber, and shade him from the sunshine of eternity." If, however, the veil is emblematic of the common plight of man, why should it isolate its wearer with a poignancy unfelt by other men and leave him lonely and alone? We have no sense in the story that all men feel as does Mr. Hooper; they are portrayed, in fact, as a cohesive band, united if only in dread of the fearful veil. Even the minister's colleague, praying by his bedside, rather cruelly misunderstands its significance. Or, on the other hand, is it possible that we can go further afield and determine that the message of the veil *is* representative and universal: that the failure to recognize it is simply the last and most chilling proof of man's imprisonment within himself? If this latter interpretation is the true one, we must conclude that Hawthorne's emphasis upon the problem as embodied in Mr. Hooper has made it impossible for him to deal with it in other characters. To achieve unity of composition his canvas can contain only one important figure. In order to present the tragic isolation of one man, Hawthorne is obliged to consider society as a solid group arrayed against his hero, ignoring for the time being the fact that this hero is Everyman.

We conclude, then, without arriving at a clear decision about the meaning of the tale, but with a sense of depths unplumbed, of rich potentialities not fully realized. The discrepancies between the two interpretations which have been outlined here must go unreconciled. Their mutual presence can, I think, be satisfactorily explained in two ways—one psychological, and one aesthetic—separable, and yet closely related. In the first place, these discrepancies represent the faculties of Hawthorne's own psychology, the heart and the head. His heart, his imagination, the inherited bent of his Puritan ancestry—all his instincts, in short—bind him in sympathy with the possessed minister, who broods over the vague and bottomless abyss of Evil. But his head, his intellect, is with the calm and steady-minded Elizabeth, who is unable to look upon the minister's vow as other than a sad but groundless whim. The ancestral Hawthorne stands beside the nineteenth-century Hawthorne in "The Minister's Black Veil," and their voices do not wholly harmonize.

Second, Hawthorne does not force a reconciliation which he has not, in Keats's words, "proved upon his pulses." Having chosen the symbol of the black veil and invented an action for it, he refrains from pushing the reader to a single conclusion. The minister himself believes the veil to be an emblem of the secret sin that poisons the souls of all mankind, but we are not compelled to accept his reading of the matter. We may, if we like, consider it rather a veil upon his understanding, whose gloomy shade conceals from the eyes behind it as much as it discloses. As it casts its shadow over the bright and various colors of the material world—colors distinct to every unhandicapped observer—so does it darken the vision of the spiritual eye.

The imagination, however, playing freely over the theme, will not content itself to remain within the limits of any single meaning. Beneath the explicit statement, the clear and simple outline of the tale, lie the irony of the minister's smile and the ambiguity of almost every incident. In "The Minister's Black Veil" the moral constitutes the framework; but it is merely an element of the completed structure.

## IV

## *"Ethan Brand"*

"HAWTHORNE," his critics say in effect, "was an inveterate allegorist. Allegory is an inferior kind of art. Hawthorne was, however, indubitably a great writer." And there the matter rests, with the implication that Hawthorne might have been greater still if he had chosen a different mode of expression. This implication may be correct: *if* he had been able to apply his genius otherwise than he did, who knows what results might have been achieved? But the speculation is a trifle barren. Hawthorne without his allegory is hard to imagine. And while the judicial critic may be quite right in regretting that Hawthorne is not Chaucer or Fielding or Balzac, to linger too long in such regret is to run the danger of forgetting his achievement. Through over-austerity we may be forced into the awkward position of condemning in theory what we admire in fact.

Allegory may become a mere tour de force in which the interest lies in clever but mechanical manipulation of thinly personified abstractions, as one occasionally finds in Spenser or in the Spenserian "Cave of Spleen" canto of *The Rape of the Lock.* Or allegory may be turned to non-literary purposes: to the service of predetermined and didactic conclusions, as in the elaborate medieval allegorical poem, or in the modern propaganda play (which is likely to be a disguised morality). On the other hand, allegory

41

has positive advantages. The purpose of creative art is to get at the essential meaning of human character, of natural objects, and of actions and processes—and allegory is a method of penetrating to their underlying significance. Allegory gives point and reference and therefore is in itself a guarantee of purpose; it affords a principle to which the action of narrative may be referred and around which the action may be organized. Skillfully handled, the presence of the allegorical double layer means an added dimension to artistic form, which should enrich rather than impoverish.

Contemporary criticism is frequently prescriptive, and the literary method it prescribes excludes Hawthorne. The formula most often approved today is scrupulously objective narration with overtones of universal meanings too elusive to be wholly captured for definition. "Symbolism" is in favor, and "allegory" is generally disapproved. This formula, however, like all such rules, ignores the complexity of the real literary situation. The world of literature is divided into various realms, governed not by any universal code, but by laws best corresponding to their individual natures and necessities. A writer, we should recall, must write what is in him; he must discover for himself the methods by which he can best express his unique view of life—which is precisely what he has to contribute. Hawthorne habitually saw things allegorically; perception of the equivalence of object and idea was, in harmony with his Puritan heritage, an organic part of his mental make-up. He could not look at a cloud, a fountain, or a cathedral without simultaneously discerning within its shape the emblem of spiritual reality. Furthermore, for Hawthorne the moral meanings of things were inseparable from their aesthetic value and significance; his creative imagination and his moral perceptions are not to be disentwined.

Hawthorne's small masterpiece "Ethan Brand," for example, is certainly open to Brownell's stricture: "His subject is always something other than its substance. Everything means something else." But "Ethan Brand" is a moving and powerful tale and one that cannot be separated from its allegorical method or even imagined apart from it. It is largely to the elaborate correspondences of the physical and spiritual, the intricate relationships set up between object and idea, that we must look for the meaning and value of the story.

In "Ethan Brand," the story of the Unpardonable Sin, almost every element—characters, action, setting, and imagery—can be accounted for in terms of an ulterior meaning without pushing ingenuity beyond the author's intention. The important characters are placed on four levels, each level representing a different relationship with an implied norm of spiritual perfection—in other words, four aspects of the human spirit. The action is simple, even bare. The hero of the tale has sought the world over for the Unpardonable Sin, only to find it at last in his own breast. He returns to the place where his quest began, to the lime-kiln beside which the conception of the Unpardonable Sin first came upon him in lonely vigils tending the fire. His mission completed, he flings himself into the burning lime pit. The setting is precisely calculated as a stage: a lonely hillside, forest-surrounded, with the lime-kiln at the center. The principal action takes place at night, in darkness shot through with lurid red from the furnace of the kiln.

As in a morality play, the characters represent varying degrees of perfection, diverging to a greater or lesser extent from an ideal of spiritual grace. Ethan Brand is, of course, immeasurably farthest from that ideal. This man, once "simple and loving," has sinned from almost inconceivable pride, which has alienated him from God and man. The Unpardonable Sin might be said to lie in the search for the Unpardonable Sin: Ethan Brand has sought to become even as the gods, knowing alike of good and evil, and he is punished for his presumption. He has "lost his hold of the magnetic chain of humanity." His intellect has come "to stand on a star-lit eminence, whither the philosophers of the earth . . . might vainly strive to clamber after him"; but his heart has correspondingly atrophied. It has "ceased to partake of the universal throb." Through pride Brand has gained knowledge without love and has desecrated the human spirit by cold and prying intellectual analysis.

Bartram the lime-burner, the present incumbent at the lime-kiln, is a dull and heavy clod. Still, he is closer to the human center than is Ethan Brand, chiefly because he lacks the impetus to depart from it. He is Ethan's foil, scornful, awed despite himself by the stupendous Unpardonable Sin, yet uncomprehending. From the nearby village Bartram calls three of Ethan Brand's old companions to view as a spectacle the Unpardonable Sin and the Sinner. These village worthies are more complex and are more densely portrayed than the simple and obtuse lime-burner. They are all specimens of mutilated and defective humanity, debased by habitual intemperance; but, unlike Brand, they have not lost all hold on the "magnetic chain." The first, a stage-agent, is somewhat faintly drawn, but he has about him a pervasive flavor and geniality, which perhaps come mainly from "brandy-toddy and tobacco-smoke." The second, Lawyer Giles, has drowned his career in liquor, until from a thriving attorney he has at length become "a soap-boiler, in a small way." Physically as well as mentally he has "come to be but the fragment of a human being, a part of one foot having been chopped off by an axe, and an entire hand torn away by the devilish grip of a steam-engine." Despite his misfortunes, however, he is not utterly lost, having "kept up the courage and spirit of a man, asked nothing in charity, and . . . fought a stern battle against want and hostile circumstances."

The third visitor is the village doctor, "a purple-visaged, rude, and brutal, yet half-gentlemanly figure, with something wild, ruined, and desperate in his talk." Like Lawyer Giles, the doctor has come close to destroying himself by liquor, "but there was supposed to be in him such wonderful skill, such native gifts of healing . . . that society caught hold of him, and would not let him sink out of its reach." These three men, in short, are profligates and sinners, but human sinners who still maintain a connection with society. By Brand they are despised as "brute beasts, that have made yourselves so, shrivelling up your souls with fiery liquors"; but their weakness is less poisonous to the spirit than is Brand's blighting strength.

Hawthorne comes closest to the ideal of spiritual grace in the figure of Bartram's son, little Joe, a timid and shrinking child. Joe is a kind of ideal observer, persistently contrasted to the persistently obtuse Bartram. Through his eyes Hawthorne presents the true interpretation of the action. Like Ethan Brand, he sees deep within men's hearts, but by sympathy and love. Brand violates the human spirit by prying into its secrets through the agency of cold, analytical intellect; little Joe apprehends it intuitively by being himself in harmony with it. At the commencement of the story the cloddish Bartram mistakes the ghastly laughter of Brand for the merry tones of a convivial drunkard, but the boy instantly senses something jarring and out of key. Again, when Ethan offers to tend the fire till morning, it is little Joe who understands. "As the boy followed his father into the hut, he looked back at the wayfarer, and the tears came into his eyes, for his tender spirit had an intuition of the bleak and terrible loneliness in which this man had enveloped himself."

The action of the tale is bare and simple, although there are unexplained overtones. It falls into three separate scenes. In the first, Ethan Brand appears at the lime-kiln, heralded by the boom of his uncanny laugh, and identifies himself to Bartram and his son. The second scene is initiated by the entrance of the three villagers, who are presently followed by a curious crowd of young men and girls. With them comes a traveling showman, "the Jew of Nuremberg," who hopes to make a profit from this fortuitous gathering by exhibiting his diorama. It is apparent that he and Ethan Brand have some occult relationship, the nature of which is not fully explained. After a time the villagers and the showman withdraw, and Brand proposes to watch by the fire till morning. Left to himself, he ascends to the top of the lime-kiln, and we see him at the climax of the tale in the act of flinging himself into the fire below.

The point of view then shifts transitionally to the sleeping lime-burner and his son, whose dreams are troubled by vague intimations of the catastrophe. "That night the sound of a fearful peal of laughter rolled heavily through the sleep of the lime-burner and his little son;

dim shapes of horror and anguish haunted their dreams, and seemed still present in the rude hovel, when they opened their eyes to the daylight." The final scene commences with the new day, in which all nature and humanity rejoice as if at the removal of some terrible threat. Brand has disappeared, but the lime-burner finds amid his newly-finished lime a human skeleton with the heart strangely converted to lime as if it had been marble. As the story ends, Bartram lifts his pole and crumbles the skeleton of Brand into fragments.

All the events are designed to provide a framework for the hero's symbolic self-destruction, to supply that act with an environment. Hawthorne is primarily interested in the Unpardonable Sin; and action, character, and setting are all devised to show it fully. Brand has completed the full circle, both physically and spiritually. He has sought the world over, and in one direction he has explored human nature to its farthest reaches. Ironically, he travels circlewise and finds his end in his beginning. The Sin is in himself. Thus his spiritual and physical journeys precisely coincide, and he returns to his point of departure, the spot where the Sin was conceived. Since his mission is fulfilled and his isolation from humanity is consummated, nothing remains but to die—a death emblematic of total separation.

If allegory is invalid, then "Ethan Brand" is unacceptable. But here, as elsewhere in Hawthorne, the method is justified by the result. There is, for instance, much pleasure to be had in tracing the methods by which everything is directed toward the center and crisis of the Unpardonable Sin.

Most prominent among the devices which bind the tale together are the recurrent references to the laugh by which Brand wordlessly expresses his unspeakable isolation and the irony of his search. This laughter, slow, heavy, and mirthless, precedes the first entrance of Brand. A little later, when Bartram inquires where the Unpardonable Sin may be, it is heard again:

> Ethan Brand laid his finger on his heart.
> "Here!" replied he.
> And then, without mirth in his countenance, but as if moved by an involuntary recognition of the infinite absurdity of seeking throughout the world for what was the closest of all things to himself, and looking into every heart, save his own, for what was hidden in no other breast, he broke into a laugh of scorn.

At the spectacle of a dog chasing his tail, Brand laughs again.

> . . . moved, it might be, by a perception of some remote analogy between his own case and that of this self-pursuing cur, he broke into the awful laugh, which, more than any other token, expressed the condition of his inward being. From that moment, the merriment of the party was at an end; they stood aghast, dreading lest the inauspicious sound should be reverberated around the horizon, and that mountain would thunder it to mountain, and so the horror be prolonged upon their ears.

The laugh tolls out for the last time in the dreams of the lime-burner and his son—Brand's final knell, filled with irony and irreconcilable defiance. The implications of this culminating outburst borrow power and spaciousness from the recurring waves of wild sound which are infrequent but regular and emphatic throughout the tale.

48

Hawthorne also employs foreshadowing to focus attention on his denouement, the self-destruction of the Unpardonable Sin. In introducing the all-important lime-kiln he remarks that it "was in nothing changed since he [Brand] *had thrown his dark thoughts into the intense glow of its furnace"*—a faint but clear warning of the climax. Again, as Ethan Brand for the first time advances into the light of the furnace fire, "he fixed his eyes—*which were very bright—intently upon the brightness of the furnace,* as if he beheld, or expected to behold, some object worthy of note within it." A little later the kinship of Brand and the fire recurs in a reference to Brand's "deeply sunken eyes, which *gleamed like fires* within the entrance of a mysterious cavern."

The prefigurement is still more definite when Brand bends forward to stir the coals and gazes into the fire. "The lime-burner sat watching him, and half suspected his strange guest of a purpose, if not to evoke a fiend, at least to plunge bodily into the flames, and thus vanish from the sight of man." Later, when the Jew of Nuremberg obscurely alludes to the Unpardonable Sin, Brand sternly bids him "Peace, . . . or get thee into the furnace yonder!" As with the laughter, this rhythmic, recurrent beat carries us powerfully forward to the inevitable end.

In the same fashion the setting and the visual imagery of the story are contrived to serve the ends of abstract allegory. First of all, Hawthorne maintains complete unity of place. The lime-kiln is the center of the action and remains so. It is described with a solidity and sharpness of outline unusual in Hawthorne, while its spiritual dimension is suggested also. "With the smoke and jets of flame issuing from the chinks and crevices of this door, which seemed to give admittance into the hillside, it resembled nothing so much as the private entrance to the infernal regions, which the shepherds of the Delectable Mountains were accustomed to show to pilgrims."

About the lime-kiln, the center of our interest, are two spheres or concentric circles of vision. The first is the area of action, illuminated by the fierce firelight when the furnace door is open. The outer sphere is the region of darkness and the unknown, encircling and cutting off the narrower realm of fire and thus bringing the lighted area into sharp emphasis and relief. The simple symmetry of this design is complicated by the occasional shutting of the furnace door, which partly darkens the inner circle and denotes a momentary slackening of action or emotional pitch. The definiteness of composition and the vivid, though generalized, imagery of Hawthorne's scene are evident in an early passage:

At frequent intervals, he [Bartram] flung back the clashing weight of the iron door, and, turning his face from the insufferable glare, thrust in huge logs of oak, or stirred the immense brands with a long pole. Within the furnace were seen the curling and riotous flames, and the burning marble, almost molten with the intensity of heat; while without, the reflection of the fire quivered on the dark intricacy of the surrounding forest, and showed in the foreground a bright and ruddy little picture of the hut, the spring beside its door, the athletic and coal-begrimed figure of the lime-burner, and the half-frightened child, shrinking into the protection of his father's shadow.

The firelight is further employed at appropriate moments to fix attention on Brand's face, the visible symbol of the Unpardonable Sin. At Brand's first appearance, "to obtain a distincter view, Bartram threw open the iron door of the kiln, whence immediately issued a gush of fierce light, that smote full upon the stranger's face and figure." Again, Brand "bent forward to gaze into the hollow prison-house of the fire, regardless of the fierce glow that reddened upon his face." And at the climax, as Brand stands with upraised arms on the top of the kiln in the act of throwing himself into the fire, "the blue flames played upon his face, and imparted the wild and ghastly light which alone could have suited its expression; it was that of a fiend on the verge of plunging into his gulf of intensest torment."

The last act of the drama of the Unpardonable Sin is thus played out against a *décor* of red and black, the appropriateness of which is sufficiently obvious. But there are other and contrasting colors. Ethan Brand is a creature of extremes; he moves without a pause from darkness into firelight. Little Joe, however, as befits his nature, is at home among tenderer hues and shrinks into the background when Brand takes the stage. As the embodiment of human love and sympathy, Joe's appearance is accompanied by moonlight and afterglow, lovely but of little power against the darkness and fire of the Unpardonable Sin: "... then reappeared the tender light of the half-full moon, which vainly strove to trace out the indistinct shapes of the neighboring mountains; and, in the upper sky, there was a flitting congregation of clouds, still faintly tinged with the rosy sunset...." This description occurs early in the evening and in the tale; as the atmosphere of the Unpardonable Sin grows more pervasive, sunset and moonlight appear no more.

This symbolic contrast is more apparent in the final scene, the morning after the tragedy, when Earth seems to rejoice at casting off an intolerable weight, a feeling shared by the sensitive child:

The early sunshine was already pouring its gold upon the mountain-tops; and though the valleys were still in shadow, they smiled cheerfully in the promise of the bright day that was hastening onward. The village, completely shut in by hills, which swelled away gently about it, looked as if it had rested peacefully in the hollow of the great hand of Providence. . . . Stepping from one to another of the clouds that rested on the hills, and thence to the loftier brotherhood that sailed in air, it seemed almost as if a mortal man might thus ascend into the heavenly regions.

To this cheerful morning scene the final and humanizing touch is added by the distant notes of a horn:

Echo caught up the notes. . . . The great hills played a concert among themselves, each contributing a strain of airy sweetness.

Little Joe's face brightened at once.

"Dear father," cried he, skipping cheerily to and fro, "that strange man is gone, and the sky and the mountains all seem glad of it!"

It appears that the human and spiritual norms are re-established and that the evils of the night are past—for the moment at least. The immense and tragic figure of Brand is gone from the scene, and, as in Shakespeare, we have tragic reconciliation with the disturbed cosmos once more tranquilized.

Thus allegory, in which "everything means something else," is a literary form wherein the spiritual and the physical are joined. The skillful overcoming of the problems which systematic allegory entails, that is, the organization of intricate detail around a central conception, is in itself a positive value.

"Ethan Brand" possesses dramatic and emotional intensity; it provides the illusion of reality necessary to ensure the suspension of disbelief; and it contains the profound depth, the tragic seriousness of Hawthorne at his best. In the somewhat pontifical words of Brownell, "Allegory justifies itself when the fiction is the fact and the moral the induction." In discussing allegory, Henry James declares that "the only case in which it is endurable is when it is extremely spontaneous, when the analogy presents itself with eager promptitude." This imaginative spontaneity is achieved, I think, in "Ethan Brand."

In this tale Hawthorne escapes the disabilities of overly consistent and mechanical allegory by two principal means: by clear and vivid projection of his imaginal symbols, particularly the lime-kiln, and by skillfully hinted complexity of character. A majority of the characters are complex in themselves, and their interrelationships are still more so. A third, less important factor is the poetry of superstition and mystery injected into the story in the figure of the Jew of Nuremberg.

The lime-kiln is the central property of the plot, and is made so by direct observation. Hawthorne gives it solidity in his description:

It was a rude, round, tower-like structure, about twenty feet high, heavily built of rough stones, and with a hillock of earth heaped about the larger part of its circumference; so that the blocks and fragments of marble might be drawn by cart-loads, and thrown in at the top. There was an opening at the bottom of the tower, like an oven-mouth, but large enough to admit a man in a stooping posture, and provided with a massive iron door. With the smoke and jets of flame issuing from the chinks and crevices of this door, which seemed to give admittance into the hillside, it resembled nothing so much as the private entrance to the infernal regions, which the shepherds of the Delectable Mountains were accustomed to show to pilgrims.

Here physical reality predominates, with allegory unobtrusively introduced in a graceful and casual-seeming allusion. Hawthorne goes on to establish his symbol firmly in time and place, to give it a kind of historical patina, a feat which he achieves with a deceptive air of relaxed ease.

Most of the characters of the tale possess at least the illusion of three-dimensional solidity, especially the three village companions, who are a complex intermixture of evil and good and produce a certain feeling of the time and spiritual wear which has produced them. With this complexity comes the still more important matter of the interrelationships of character in "Ethan Brand," which soften and enrich the firm outlines of the allegory. The general meaning of the story presents no difficulty. The hero has sinned through inordinate and inhuman pride of intellect, and he receives a fitting punishment. But within the broad design there is human uncertainty, flexibility of relationship, and ambiguity of emphasis. Hawthorne is Christian in loving the sinner while he hates the sin; he has, it may be, put too much of himself into Ethan Brand to view him with complete disfavor. Hawthorne is not minatory; despite the moral he does not himself occupy the seat of judgment. Ethan Brand, who has cast himself away by his own choice, is frequently more admirable than the inferior sinners about him. It is impossible not to sympathize with Brand when he returns to his native village, an artist of the perverse, but still an artist. Ironically enough, the import of his burden is totally beyond the comprehension of all but little Joe, who perceives it intuitively. Brand is beaten by the Philistinism of the village, which even the spectacle of the Unpardonable Sin fails to impress beyond a momentary superstitious dread.

At times, then, we participate with Brand in his encounters with the duller normal, and it is Hawthorne's intention that we should. He underlines the brutishness of Bartram with persistent iteration. Bartram is first introduced to us as "a rough, heavy-looking man." A few paragraphs later he becomes an "obtuse middle-aged clown." After remarking that the business of tending the fire is a lonesome, "and, when the character is inclined to thought . . . an intensely thoughtful occupation," Hawthorne tells us that Bartram "troubled himself with no thoughts save the very few that were requisite to his business." Furthermore, the lime-burner at the outset ludicrously misapprehends the purport of the dreadful laugh and a few moments later callously orders his son to " 'scamper down to the tavern in the village, and tell the jolly fellows there that Ethan Brand has come back, and that he has found the Unpardonable Sin!' "

The "jolly fellows," when they appear, show the same incomprehension.

These three worthies pressed forward, and greeted Ethan Brand each after his own fashion, earnestly inviting him to partake of the contents of a certain black bottle, in which, as they averred, he would find something far better worth seeking than the Unpardonable Sin. No mind, which has wrought itself by intense and solitary meditation into a high state of enthusiasm, can endure the kind of contact with low and vulgar modes of thought and feeling to which Ethan Brand was now subjected. It made him doubt—and, strange to say, it was a painful doubt—whether he had indeed found the Unpardonable Sin, and found it within himself. The whole question on which he had exhausted life, and more than life, looked like a delusion.

Surely our feelings—and Hawthorne's—are here on the side of Brand. The pattern is completed as the drunken doctor jeers at him: " 'You have no more found the Unpardonable Sin than yonder boy Joe has. You are but a crazy fellow,—I told you so twenty years ago,—neither better nor worse than a crazy fellow. . . !' "

At the conclusion the complete insensitivity of Bartram evokes the same reaction:

The marble was all burnt into perfect, snow-white lime. But on its surface, in the midst of the circle,—snow-white too, and thoroughly converted into lime,—lay a human skeleton, in the attitude of a person who, after long toil, lies down to long repose. Within the ribs—strange to say—was the shape of a human heart.

"Was the fellow's heart made of marble?" cried Bartram, in some perplexity at this phenomenon. "At any rate, it is burnt into what looks like special good lime; and, taking all the bones together, my kiln is half a bushel the richer for him."

So saying, the rude lime-burner lifted his pole, and, letting it fall upon the skeleton, the relics of Ethan Brand were crumbled into fragments.

This is without doubt in part a moralistic reflection of Hawthorne's—*vanitas vanitatum,* this is the end of pride and misguided ambition—but it is also a reflection upon the lime-burner.

The significance of "Ethan Brand" does not lie, then, simply in the praise of the normal, for in this instance the normal is not always attractive. The story will not bear the burden of a simple meaning. Little Joe represents the ideal, but he is too faintly drawn to be fully convincing. He is a child and an observer only, and his perfection is too fortuitous and too insecure to counterbalance the weight of the demoniac Brand. Fully to realize the ideal a larger, more substantial character would be necessary, one who held his virtue upon a more certain tenure.

This hinted ambivalence of character relationship is not a defect but an essential quality in the story. It is the element of flexibility and variety by means of which Hawthorne is able to do justice to the complex situations. By its use he escapes the invidious position of the puppet-master and gives his characters the appearance of autonomy of action. Through it he is able to remain true to art and imagination while dealing with a moral theme. For in "Ethan Brand" he tells us, not "Be good, or suffer the consequences," but rather, "This is what must happen under these circumstances," and "Here but for the grace of God go I." Character is allowed free play, and the potentialities of the situation are given room to develop.

Ambiguity and a certain unexpectedness are enhanced by deliberate poetic mystery in some particulars. In contrast to the fierce light of the inner circle, the outer ring of darkness hints at the unknown region beyond the limits of moral certainty. There is also the effect of the alternate opening and closing of the furnace door, by which clear moral vision is at intervals obscured and misled. Moreover, there is a touch in the showman's exhibition which artfully hints at uncertainty, at unexplored ambiguity of action. First Hawthorne describes the distorted view of the showman's hand amid the pictures in the diorama: "Some purported to be cities, public edifices, and ruined castles in Europe; others represented Napoleon's battles and Nelson's sea fights; and in the midst of these would be seen a gigantic, brown, hairy hand,—which might have been mistaken for the Hand of Destiny, though in truth, it was only the showman's. . . ." This effect is repeated when little Joe puts his head into the box. "Viewed through the magnifying-glasses, the boy's round, rosy visage assumed the strangest imaginable aspect of an immense Titanic child, the mouth grinning broadly, and the eyes and every other feature overflowing with fun at the joke." A quick shift follows when the child sees Ethan Brand watching him through the glass and turns pale with horror.

The figure of the showman has a picturesqueness which opens the way to a new dimension in the tale, a warmly fantastic vista of superstition and legend which has been sanctioned and humanized by long and widespread use. On the one hand the showman is Ethan Brand's familiar spirit—according to local belief a demon who lived amid "the intensest element of fire" in the lime-kiln furnace. He is also, however, the Wandering Jew, who brings with him the fascination and power of myth and legend.

V

## *"The Maypole of Merry Mount"*

By using the Coleridgean distinction between "allegory" and "symbol," a distinction widely used at present, it is possible to describe what happens in a Hawthorne tale containing both elements. However, the procedure which follows runs counter to the current tendency to define the quality of a writer's whole production within these terms, an obvious example of which is the custom, now a sort of easy, habitual cant, of distinguishing between the "allegory" of Hawthorne and the "symbolism" of Melville—a distinction which is always made to Hawthorne's discredit.

In his prefatory note to "The Maypole of Merry Mount" Hawthorne remarks that "there is an admirable foundation for a philosophical romance in the curious history of the early settlement of Mount Wollaston, or Merry Mount. In the slight sketch here attempted, the facts, recorded on the grave pages of our New England annalists, have wrought themselves, almost spontaneously, into a sort of allegory." The terms of this allegory he states in a single sentence in the opening paragraph of the story: "Jollity and gloom were contending for an empire." The allegorical element of "The Maypole of Merry Mount" resides in the clear-cut statement and development of a problem, which is embodied in the conflict between Merry Mount and Plymouth, jollity and gloom, Merry England and Puritan New England. The Puritans defeat the joyous colonists, of course, with only the semblance of a struggle. "As the moral gloom of the world overpowers all systematic gayety, even so was their home of wild mirth made desolate amid the sad forest." The core of the story lies in a conflict between abstractions, and the outcome is determined in accordance with an assumption about the world and reality. The dour Puritan triumphs because he is in tune with the nature of things.

Within this broad allegorical framework every image and particular takes its assigned place. It may be useful to describe the allegorical organization differently. The conflicting elements which constitute the plot are magnetic poles, each with its field of images and characters. The central symbol of Merry Mount is the Maypole; it has its counterpart in "the Puritan Maypole," the whipping post. The colonists of Merry Mount are creatures of light; "they stood in the broad smile of sunset." The essence of Puritan power is dark. ". . . the men of iron shook their heads and frowned so darkly that the revellers looked up, imagining that a momentary cloud had overcast the sunshine, which was to be perpetual there." This contrast reveals still a further contrast: the Puritans are "men of iron . . . each with a horseload of iron armor to burden his footsteps"; the colonists are "silken," light-footed. "Light had their footsteps been on land, and as lightly they came across the sea." Their lives are a dance: "The Lord and Lady of the May . . . were really and truly to be partners for the dance of life, beginning the measure that same bright eve." For the Puritans the whip is the only appropriate call to the dance. Says Endicott, the arch-Puritan, " 'I thought not to repent me of cutting down a Maypole . . . yet now I could find in my heart to plant it again, and give each of these bestial pagans one other dance about their idol.' " He admonishes the Lord and Lady of the May, " 'Nor think ye, young ones, that they are the happiest, even in our lifetime of a moment, who misspend it in dancing round a Maypole.' " The antithesis of Plymouth and Merry Mount Hawthorne distills into four sentences:

When they [the Puritans] met in conclave, it was never to keep up the old English mirth, but to hear sermons three hours long, or to proclaim bounties on the heads of wolves and the scalps of Indians. Their festivals were fast days, and their chief past-time the singing of psalms. Woe to the youth or maiden who did but dream of a dance! The selectman nodded to the constable; and there sat the light-heeled reprobate in the stocks; or if he danced, it was round the whipping-post, which might be termed the Puritan Maypole.

For an adequate description of the structure of allegory in "The Maypole of Merry Mount" we must resort to another shift in focus, which brings "The Lord and Lady of the May" into the foreground. This youthful pair, whose wedding feast is rudely broken off by Puritan violence, are "a new Adam and Eve" suddenly thrust forth from Paradise. " 'The troubles of life have come hastily on this young couple,' observed Endicott." They are symbols of humanity, forced to choose between the "systematic gayety" of Merry Mount and the "moral gloom" of the Puritans. That they are constrained by force to accept the gloom is in itself significant. The couple, sensitive and acute spirits who represent the moral norm of the story and typify the keenest human insight, find themselves forced to make their choice by an overwhelming power, which is not merely external. Puritanism lies closer to truth than does the paradise of Merry Mount.

"The Maypole of Merry Mount" is therefore an allegory; it is constructed on a conflict of moral abstractions with a predetermined conclusion, and it functions consistently on two levels of meaning. All particular images, characters, actions, and situations possess their abstract equivalents. Moreover, by shifting the emphasis of meaning to the principal characters, we can restate the theme as the conflict of the human spirit aroused by the necessity of making a moral choice. Yet this analysis has not dealt fully with all the issues raised by the allegorical element itself. This inadequacy can perhaps be remedied by discussing the story as symbol.

As allegory, "The Maypole of Merry Mount" presents the virtues of creative power and penetration through which Hawthorne succeeds in endowing far-reaching historical, cultural, and moral issues with form and point. There is virtue also in the economy and symmetry of design to which the allegorical purpose gives rise. It gives the initial impulse for shaping relationships between characters and events through the necessity of recreating or reshaping the historical sources of the tale. Therefore we shall look to the allegory as the fountainhead of much or most of the conscious craftsmanship and artistry of the story, which is made up of such elements as the objectification of the love of pleasure in the Maypole, and of the spirit of Puritanism in the sword which fells it:

And with his keen sword Endicott assaulted the hallowed Maypole. Nor long did it resist his arm. It groaned with a dismal sound; it showered leaves and rosebuds upon the remorseless enthusiast; and finally, with all its green boughs and ribbons and flowers, symbolic of departed pleasures, down fell the banner staff of Merry Mount.

However, allegory alone, in the restricted sense to which we generally confine the term, is inadequate to characterize Hawthorne's tale, because it presupposes a greater interest in the moral meaning of a story than in the story itself and because it demands a simpler, more sharply outlined problem and solution than suits with a convincing imitation of reality.

Here the element of "symbol" enters to supplement allegory. If we accept the terms of the allegorical statement of theme in "The Maypole of Merry Mount," we get either a thin and conventional solution or an unresolved conflict—on the one hand an Aesop's fable of the ant and the grasshopper, and on the other a sharp and raw cleavage, since while Hawthorne's sympathies are with the Merry Mounters he is constrained to let the Puritans win by history itself and by his own sense of probability.

Allegory is deductive; the writer commences with a preconceived problem and solution and fits his characters and action to them. Symbol is inductive; if a writer has succeeded in choosing such characters, action, and symbols as awaken his own interest and creative imagination, he follows where they lead him, to some extent. He considers their inherent laws, since these grow from the situation and from his own feelings; and the meaning of his story emerges organically from the workings of these elements. Thus the resolution of the problem may be drawn from the characters and their action; even though they have been formulated to carry out a predetermined plan, at a certain point they take over and provide the conclusion themselves. In "The Maypole of Merry Mount" the two poles of the problem gain control and win at least a semi-independence as soon as Hawthorne considers them in the round and they begin to develop concretely in an actual, particular situation. When his imagination releases them from abstraction they take on the complexity of life.

It would be an overstatement to say that in "The Maypole of Merry Mount" Hawthorne achieves a complete resolution on all levels. Its problem reveals a cleavage in his vision of reality which he could not overcome. While it has been argued, and may be true, that his Lord and Lady of the May represent a golden mean between the extremes of Merry Mount and Plymouth, the solution which they present is doctrinal rather than imaginative. Hawthorne intellectually points the way, but he does not realize it in the story. In his conclusion one sentence holds out the hope of synthesis: ". . . as their flowery garland was wreathed of the brightest roses that had grown there, so, in the tie that united them, were intertwined all the purest and best of their early joys." The hope is all too frail, however. The lovers are absorbed by Plymouth and Puritanism; their fate is a surrender to values imperfect and incomplete.

There is present, however, an imaginative resolution of tone and feeling which arises from Hawthorne's honest and full acceptance of the complexity of the problem. Without question his sympathies are with Merry Mount. But the Puritans are closer to reality, the world *is* a place of moral gloom, darkened with the curse of Adam. Merry

Mount possesses only a dream. Yet this dream is not merely one of coarse revelry; it is the dream of play, of art, of imagination. It is fallacious in that the dreamers leave out too much of their whole experience. They hold a pleasant harvest feast, but their crop is "of the smallest." They imitate and abstract from life without living. The Puritans are incomplete in the opposite direction. They perceive the burden of life and mistake it for the whole of reality.

The commencement of the tale is a poetic celebration of Merry Mount, which goes quite beyond the functional requirements of the allegory. This "gay colony" dwells in perpetual May, and its central symbol, the venerated Maypole, is an object of aesthetic contemplation as well as an emblem of allegory. "Garden flowers, and blossoms of the wilderness, laughed gladly forth amid the verdure, so fresh and dewy that they must have grown by magic on that happy pine-tree." In the entire passage is an intense wistfulness, an emotion embodied in rich and elaborately cadenced prose, which betrays a special love for Merry Mount. "O, people of the Golden Age, the chief of your husbandry was to raise flowers!"

This sentence gives a clue to the source of Hawthorne's emotion. Merry Mount is the dream of paradise, the myth of the Golden Age, of Man before the Fall. In many respects the colony is sanctioned and supported by Nature itself, decked in the pageantry of the seasons. The life of Merry Mount is a hymn to life, a poetic ritual.

... what chiefly characterized the colonists of Merry Mount was their veneration for the Maypole. It has made their true history a poet's tale. Spring decked the hallowed emblem with young blossoms and fresh green boughs; Summer brought roses of the deepest blush, and the perfected foliage of the forest; Autumn enriched it with that red and yellow gorgeousness which converts each wildwood leaf into a painted flower; and Winter silvered it with sleet, and hung it round with icicles, till it flashed in the cold sunshine, itself a frozen sunbeam.

In the composition of the scene allegory is supplemented by symbol. The necessary properties and actions of the story are organized and governed by the allegory. As is appropriate, the Maypole, a tall pine, is the visual center of the scene. Facing it stand the Lord and Lady of the May and the English priest, "canonically dressed, yet decked with flowers, in heathen fashion." These chief figures are ringed about with a "wild throng" of followers, disguised as beasts, clowns, Indians, and figures of heraldry. A live bear stands hand in hand with them: "His inferior nature rose half way, to meet his companions as they stooped." The revellers are likened to "the crew of Comus, some already transformed to brutes, some midway between man and beast, and the others rioting in the flow of tipsy jollity that foreran the change." Unknown to themselves, they are being watched by a band of Puritans, concealed near by in the forest.

In the midst of the gaiety Edith, the Lady of the May, is mysteriously saddened, an emotion inappropriate at Merry Mount. "From the moment that they truly loved, they had subjected themselves to earth's doom of care and sorrow, and troubled joy. . . ." The waning of Merry Mount is the waning of sunlight. As the last sunbeam fades from the summit of the Maypole, "evening gloom" rushes "instantaneously from the black surrounding woods." Amid the black shadows stand the dark Puritans, who are masters of the situation within a few moments. Breaking the ordered pattern of Merry Mount, they immediately form a new one. "The leader of the hostile party stood in the center of the circle, while the rout of monsters cowered around him, like evil spirits in the presence of a dread magician." The leader, Endicott, hews down the Maypole, the revelers are condemned to whippings, the stocks, and imprisonment, and the Lord and Lady of the May stand powerless before their stern judge. They are forgiven their transgressions at the cost of adoption into the Puritan society. Symbolically, Endicott calls for "garments of a more decent fashion" to clothe the couple, and commands that the young man's hair be cut forthwith.

Thus every particular is systematically employed in the service of allegory. But Hawthorne's visual composition is also an aesthetic design in itself. Its careful groupings and proportions, its focusing and arrangement of detail, its use of color-contrasts and color themes (the rainbow Maypole, for example, repeated in the rainbow scarf of the May Lord), its blend as well as contrast of light—all these elements are unfunctional to allegory, although they are not necessarily incompatible with it. In other particulars the elements of allegory and symbol mingle more closely. It has been suggested earlier that Hawthorne achieves a reconciliation of tone and feeling. This reconciliation is attained in part by skillful and steady modification of the early praise of Merry Mount, which prepares us for its destruction. The effect of the colonists' disguises, the Comus masques, is of course to lower the colonists in our esteem. They are given a kind of standing, however, when they are likened to fauns and nymphs, who "when driven from their classic groves and homes of ancient fable, had sought refuge, as all the persecuted did, in the fresh woods of the West." In general, too, they are objects of pleasure and wonder, intended for our enjoyment and not for our reprehension. Thus they cannot be accounted for by allegory alone.

The dreamlike, phantasmagoric atmosphere with which Hawthorne invests his scene and actors is also unrelated to allegory. The aura of dream is ambivalent even on the level of allegory. It emphasizes the unreality of Merry Mount, but it stands for our longing as well. "Through a world of toil and care she [May] flitted with a dreamlike smile, and came hither to find a home. . . ." It is also an element of aesthetic pleasure, a deliberate and playful mystification which delights in itself.

Thus when the story goes beyond the necessities of its theme, when its particulars are not merely functional, it becomes symbol as well as allegory. It may be useful to compare this distinction to John Crowe Ransom's distinction between *structure* and *texture,* in which the structure, or the conceptual framework, is supplemented by the rich particularity of texture, functionally unnecessary but containing within itself the specific literary value of the work—that substance which differentiates literature from exposition or argument. Or we may say with Coleridge that Hawthorne is interested in the Maypole not merely as a part of the whole—that is, as an element of the allegory—but also as an aesthetic and imaginative whole in itself.

Allegory and symbol are not, of course, to be separated in Hawthorne, except for purposes of analysis. Their operations are simultaneous and are organically united. Allegory is the essential element of the Hawthorne tales, yet allegory is nevertheless incomplete without the addition of symbol. The two represent, perhaps, the co-operation of conscious and unconscious artistry, in which the achievement of symbol is the reward for the effort of allegory. It is only through hard and discriminating exercise of intellect that the imagination is set to work and the unified whole is produced.

# VI

# *"The Artist of the Beautiful"*

ONE IS TEMPTED to describe "The Artist of
the Beautiful" as an aesthetic *Pilgrim's Progress*, in which the artist journeys his difficult road toward
salvation, struggling through his Slough of Despond,
combating his Giant Despair, overcoming his fiend Apol-
lyon, until after many days he reaches the Heavenly
City prepared for him. Owen Warland, the artist, is a
watchmaker who strives to embody the pure idea of the
beautiful in the form of a marvelously wrought artificial
butterfly, a "spiritualized mechanism" strangely imbued
by his imagination with a mysterious life of its own. Before he succeeds in consummating his imaginative conception he is forced to do battle with the mass of his
society, which not only misunderstands but even actively
condemns his purposes. This society is represented by
three persons: Peter Hovenden, his old master; Hovenden's daughter Annie, whom Warland loves; and Robert
Danforth, a herculean blacksmith, who wins Annie when
Warland fails. The plot of "The Artist of the Beautiful"
is the artist's struggle with these three friendly enemies,
each of whom seeks to turn him from his purpose.

This plot consists of a series of oppositions. The
broadest and simplest of these is Warland's disinterested
search for the beautiful against the criteria of utility and
self-interest assumed by his society. He has always been

"remarkable for a delicate ingenuity. . . . But it was always for purposes of grace, and never with any mockery of the useful." Society has attempted without success to assimilate this rebel from its laws. "The boy's relatives saw nothing to be done—as perhaps there was not—than to bind him apprentice to a watchmaker, hoping that his strange ingenuity might thus be regulated and put to utilitarian purposes." Society's verdict on his art is uttered by the blacksmith Danforth, who is naïvely definitive. In the concluding scene of the story Annie inquires whether Warland's marvelous butterfly is actually alive, so perfect an imitation is it of life. " 'Alive? To be sure it is,' " answers Danforth. " 'Do you suppose any mortal has skill enough to make a butterfly, or would put himself to the trouble of making one, when any child may catch a score of them in a summer's afternoon?' "

The second opposition devolves from the contrast of Warland's idealism with society's materialism—the latter appearing in different aspects in the various characters of Hovenden, Danforth, and Annie. Warland is a highly transcendental artist, who seeks to embody "the beautiful idea" in his butterfly. Peter Hovenden is a cold materialist, whose mere presence is blighting to Warland's imagination. "There was nothing so antipodal to his nature as this man's cold, unimaginative sagacity, by contact with which everything was converted into a dream except the densest matter of the physical world." Danforth represents another, more innocent aspect of materialism; whereas Hovenden is keen enough to hate (he has "just enough of penetration to torture Owen's soul with the bitterness of worldly criticism"), Danforth is merely puzzled and amused by the artist's aspirations. His spiritual impact on the sensitive artist is hardly less damaging, however, than the effect of Hovenden. A "man of main strength," he is intolerable to the delicate organization of Warland. " 'He would drive me mad were I to meet him often. His hard, brute force darkens and confuses the spiritual element within me. . . .' " The case of Annie Hovenden is more difficult to define. Possessing sufficient insight to delude Warland into believing her a kindred spirit, she yet lacks the talisman which would admit her to his inmost thought. With much kindliness, she feels a veiled contempt for Warland and his unreal quest for ideal beauty. Her marriage to Danforth, the man of earth and iron, is perhaps sufficient to account for her.

From this general antithesis of ideal and material arise three other oppositions in "The Artist of the Beautiful," each with its special emphasis and importance: time and eternity, understanding and imagination, and mechanism and organism. All of these concern primarily the relationship between Warland and Peter Hovenden.

In the opening scene of the story we are shown Warland's shop window. A number of watches are displayed within, "all with their faces turned from the streets, as if churlishly disinclined to inform the wayfarers what o'clock it was." This is a fitting introduction to the rebel watchmaker, of whose ingenuity Hovenden scornfully exclaims, " 'All the effect that ever I knew of it was to spoil the accuracy of some of the best watches in my shop.' " Warland, in fact, behaves toward Time with a levity which his society finds intolerable:

. . . when his apprenticeship was served out, and he had taken the little shop which Peter Hovenden's failing eyesight compelled him to relinquish, then did people recognize how unfit a person was Owen Warland to lead old blind Father Time along his daily course. One of his most rational projects was to connect a musical operation with the machinery of his watches, so that all the harsh dissonances of life might be rendered tuneful, and each flitting moment fall into the abyss of the past in golden drops of harmony. . . . Several freaks of this kind quite destroyed the young watchmaker's credit with that steady and matter-of-fact class of people who hold the opinion that time is not to be trifled with. . . .

When through the agency of Hovenden the artist temporarily loses his creative power, the loss manifests itself in a sudden devotion to the task of the watchmaker: "It was marvellous to witness the obtuse gravity with which he would inspect the wheels of a great old silver watch." So closely does Warland apply himself to business that at length he is invited by general consent to regulate the clock in the church steeple, a commission which he executes to perfection. To the mind of Hovenden, Time's devotee, the change is wholly for the better. He even proposes to Warland that he should " 'doctor this precious old watch of mine; though, except my daughter Annie, I have nothing else so valuable in the world.' " On Warland's disclaiming his worthiness, Hovenden replies with a strange ambiguity. " 'In time,' said the latter,—'in time, you will be capable of it.' " If Warland had consented to undertake this crucial task, one must suppose that his subjection to the tyranny of Time would have been irremediable; but he refuses and leaves a way open to freedom.

Warland the idealist and artist is a symbol of imagination, Hovenden the materialist a symbol of understanding, or analytical reason. The opposition is explicit and is clearly perceived by the sensitive Warland. "Owen never met this man without a shrinking of the heart. Of all the world he was most terrible, by reason of a keen understanding which saw so distinctly what it did see, and disbelieved so uncompromisingly in what it could not see." Amid the various tribulations which beset him, Owen for a time himself declines into the mental state of Hovenden. He loses his "faith in the invisible" and falls so far as to pride himself in his skepticism. "This," says Hawthorne, "is the calamity of men whose spiritual part dies out of them and leaves the grosser understanding to assimilate them more and more to the things of which it alone can take cognizance. . . ." In Warland, however, this state is a sleep from which he awakens, to become once more a "being of thought, imagination, and keenest sensibility."

In the conclusion of "The Artist of the Beautiful" the conflict between understanding and imagination is crucial. Warland, successful in embodying his imaginative vision in the miraculous butterfly, brings it as a gift to Annie, now long a matron. Hovenden is present at the scene, together with Annie and Danforth and their infant child. The insect, mysteriously alive, flutters from one person to another at the command of the artist. It is immediately clear that Hovenden is inimical to its being; his mocking unbelief is subtly destructive.

"Let us see," said Peter Hovenden, rising from his chair, with a sneer upon his face that always made people doubt, as he himself did, in everything but a material existence. "Here is my finger for it to alight upon. *I shall understand it better when once I have touched it.*"

At his touch the insect droops and instantly loses its luminous vitality. Warland calmly explains this phenomenon: " 'In an atmosphere of doubt and mockery its exquisite susceptibility suffers torture, as does the soul of him who instilled his own life into it.' "

And indeed, understanding succeeds in destroying the creature of imagination, though imagination itself emerges unscathed and triumphant. In an attempt to repair the effects of its contact with Hovenden, Annie delivers the butterfly over to its worst enemy—her child. This child, still a baby, is yet a reincarnation of the spirit of Hovenden and is all the more destructive because as yet he is unrestrained by social decency. Warland recognizes him at first sight: ". . . the artist was disturbed by the child's look, as imagining a resemblance between it and Peter Hovenden's habitual expression." The child seizes the butterfly and crushes it in his fingers. Understanding has taken its due tribute; what is subject to the senses it must command. But nevertheless, victory lies with Warland and imagination. "He had caught a far other butterfly than this. When the artist rose high enough to achieve the beautiful, the symbol by which he made it perceptible to mortal senses became of little value in his eyes while his spirit possessed itself in the enjoyment of the reality."

Warland's creation, although a mechanism, transcends the merely mechanical to become a living organism. The artist of the beautiful is a consummate mechanic who is yet unsatisfied with the purposes of mechanism. Danforth's blundering suggestion that he must be " 'trying to discover the perpetual motion' " merely disgusts Warland. Perpetual motion, he replies, is " 'a dream that may delude men whose brains are mystified with matter, but not me.' " Decisively he disposes of the question: " 'I am not ambitious to be honored with the paternity of a new kind of cotton machine.' " His real purpose is divined in part by a momentary insight on the part of Annie Hovenden: Owen is " 'taken up with the notion of putting spirit into machinery.' " Later the artist enlarges upon this hint. In his thought life, beauty, and ideality are one. He has considered it "possible, in a certain sense, to spiritualize machinery, and to combine with the new species of life and motion thus produced a beauty that should attain to the ideal which Nature has proposed to herself in all her creatures, but has never taken pains to realize."

This aspiration Warland successfully embodies in *his* creature: "Nature's ideal butterfly was here realized in all its perfection." It is organic, mysteriously vitalized. "The rich down was visible upon its wings; the lustre of its eyes seemed instinct with spirit." It glistens with a radiance of its own. Annie, now married to Danforth, asks the crucial question, which poses the whole problem of "organic unity" and the "life" of a work of art. " 'Tell me if it be alive,' " she demands, " 'or whether you created it.' " The artist's answer, though paradoxical, is also inevitable. " '. . . it may well be said to possess life, for it has absorbed my own being into itself; and in the secret of that butterfly, and in its beauty,—which is not merely outward, but deep as its whole system,—is represented the intellect, the imagination, the sensibility, the soul of an Artist of the Beautiful!' "

In "The Artist of the Beautiful" Hawthorne expounds the fundamental ethic, metaphysic, psychology, and aesthetic of English Romanticism. The antitheses of ideal-material, time-eternity, understanding-imagination, and mechanism-organism are pervasively present in all the great Romantic poets. Most fully and philosophically developed in Coleridge, they are also to be found in different degrees and various interpretations in Wordsworth, Shelley, Keats, and even Byron. The germ of Romantic doctrine is transcendental idealism and the Platonic belief in the ultimate identity of Goodness, Truth, and Beauty. This doctrine in its Romantic form is calculated to glorify the artist as the moral sage of all men and as the repositor and revealer of Beauty and Truth. Conversely but logically enough it tends also to isolate the artist by his very possession of a perception so largely unknown and uncredited by the mass of mankind that their attitude towards him is likely to be an odd and complex mixture of reverence, distrust, scorn, and amusement. And since his values, based as they are upon the unseen ideal, are largely a reversal of the utilitarian values of everyday existence, he will be despised by the insensitive in almost direct ratio to his real merits.

The relation of these remarks to "The Artist of the Beautiful" is evident. Understanding is the faculty by which we perceive the world as Material—utilitarian, abstractive, and divisive, understanding is indispensable but incomplete. Through it alone, the world is essentially dead and meaningless; and the mass of men view reality with the aid of understanding only. Imagination, on the other hand, perceives the ideal, which is the innate reality and truth of things. Imagination endows the world with life and unity, and consequently with meaning. Understanding permits only

> *... that inanimate cold world allowed*
> *To the poor loveless ever-anxious crowd,*

77

while through imagination we see "into the life of things," beholding

*A motion and a spirit that impels*
*All thinking things, all objects of all thought,*
*And rolls through all things.*

The mechanical is the unfortunate result of applying the unaided understanding to the creation of art. Understanding, which imitates the inadequate reality to which it is confined, produces a merely mechanical work, an uninspired arrangement of inert and predetermined materials. In the context of 'The Artist of the Beautiful" the mechanical is the art of the watchmaker who, unlike Warland, sticks to his trade. The imagination, perceiving in reality the ideal, the basic life principle, and unity, reproduces them in art, endowing the individual work with such life and organic unity as is possible and appropriate to it. It follows, then, that the imaginative work of art will be a living organism with a development and an individuality appropriate to the laws inherent in itself and in its kind. Natural, yet superior to Nature in that it embodies Nature's essence, it magically combines the ideal with the particular. Such a work is the butterfly of Owen Warland.

"The Artist of the Beautiful" is a Romantic affirmation of the value of art and of the spiritual pre-eminence of the artist's imagination, which intuitively penetrates to highest Goodness, Truth, and Beauty. In this story belief, idealism, and love of beauty are exalted by being contrasted with materialist skepticism and mere utility. Let us now shift the focus of the narrative to describe these oppositions in different terms, this time emphasizing the artist's dedicated effort to carry out his task. From this point of view the basic symbol is an exquisite mechanism, almost tragically susceptible to the slightest jar. This "delicate piece of mechanism" is immediately set before us in the opening scene, in which Hovenden and his daughter watch Warland through the shop window as he bends earnestly over his creation. Warland's mechanism represents the problem of the work of art, and the movement of the story is the movement of its fortunes. It stands also for Warland himself, and both must surmount the hostility of the world, which is represented to us in the figures of Hovenden, Danforth, and Annie.

The mere perception of Annie's presence is sufficient to banish the poise of the artist. " 'I shall scarcely,' " says Warland, " 'be able to work again on this exquisite mechanism tonight.' " The rude strength of Danforth has a more violent influence. The uproar of his laughter causes Owen and the bell glasses on his cupboard (also symbols of fragile organization and balance) to quiver in unison, and when the artist returns to his work his first stroke ruins the mechanism and nullifies the labor of many months. " 'The vapor, the influence of that brute force,— it has bewildered me and obscured my perception.' " In his next trial Peter Hovenden threatens to destroy the mechanism—" 'See! with one pinch of my finger and thumb I am going to deliver you from all future peril' " —and so agitates Warland as to stop the work once more. Annie Hovenden attacks him more subtly, and more successfully because of her partial insight into his purposes. Warland is on the point of confiding in her when she destroys everything by carelessly toying with the vital mechanism. She gives it but "the slightest possible touch, with the point of a needle," but it is sufficient. She has trifled frivolously with his deepest yet most vulnerable sensibilities. And Annie has one more blow to strike, the heaviest of all. At Hovenden's announcement of her engagement to Danforth the artist seems unmoved, but "One slight outbreak, however, imperceptible to the old watchmaker, he allowed himself. Raising the instrument with which he was about to begin his work, he let it fall upon the little system of machinery that had, anew, cost him months of thought and toil. It was shattered by the stroke!"

The framework of Hawthorne's fiction is customarily a doctrine, a belief, or a moral proposition which he proceeds to test by using his imagination. The theme of *The Scarlet Letter* is the damage to the soul from sin, but the theme itself is tried to the utmost and is exposed to unrelenting scrutiny. The characters have leave to range; no possibility of escape from the grim prison of the sin is left unexplored; no evidence, though contrary to the novel's thesis, is slighted or suppressed. It is even suggested that sin itself is illusory and that the adultery of Hester and Dimmesdale has brought forth good instead of evil: doctrines which are to be taken as quite contrary to the book's true purport. *The Marble Faun* is another case in point. Its narrative is solidly based upon the doctrine of the fall of man. Miriam and Donatello have sinned and must pay the penalty morally, psychologically, and socially. Yet Hawthorne in one crucial instance casts doubt on the reality of free will and personal responsibility and in another seems to argue strongly that the ultimate consequences of Donatello's crime must actually be beneficial.

So Hawthorne also tests the theme of "The Artist of

the Beautiful" and furnishes material for other interpretations than his own. His characters may and should be read allegorically both as types and as ideas, but they become complex human beings as well, creatures of mingled strength and weakness, good and evil. The four figures of the tale can be labeled as types. Warland is the artist, Hovenden the businessman, Danforth the common man, and Annie—shall we say—the domestic woman. Or they may be considered as abstract ideas, so that Warland now becomes the quest for the ideal, Hovenden cynicism or materialism (in Hawthorne much the same thing), Danforth physical strength, and Annie the world's temptations. But they are also men and women, appealing and repellent alike, good often and bad as well. Their conflicts and relationships, however clear the ultimate verdict, are frequently complex and ambivalent.

Of Warland's three antagonists Peter Hovenden is plainly the least amiable and the worst, a soul-blighting cynic and materialist; and yet his nature has a commonsense centrality which is worthy of respect. In his character is a tenacious clutch upon a harsh reality, a steady grasp upon the doom of Adam. " '. . . give me the worker in iron after all is said and done,' " says he. " 'He spends his labor upon a reality.' " Toward Warland he feels "the mixture of contempt and indignation which mankind, of whom he was partly a representative, deem themselves entitled to feel towards all simpletons who seek other prizes than the dusty one along the highway." Seen from Hovenden's point of view the idealist Warland seems weak and frail, his vision of reality a deluded optimism, his delicate intuition a reaching among shadows.

We may get at the quality of Hovenden by placing him among his fictional family, a group of characters

81

present throughout Hawthorne's work. He closely resembles the nameless Cynic of "The Great Carbuncle," who "was chiefly distinguished by a sneer that always contorted his thin visage, and by a prodigious pair of spectacles, which were supposed to deform and discolor the whole face of nature, to this gentleman's perception." The Cynic is almost wholly bad and comes to a very bad end. Doffing his spectacles in scornful skepticism, he looks full upon the Great Carbuncle and is blasted by its light. "So long accustomed to view all objects through a medium that deprived them of every glimpse of brightness, a single flash of so glorious a phenomenon, striking upon his naked vision, had blinded him forever." Hovenden likewise bears a family resemblance to Westervelt, the mesmerist villain of *The Blithedale Romance*, whose evil lies in no positive trait or spiritual bent, but simply in an all-embracing materialism which negates all moral meaning. The suicide of the brilliant and passionate Zenobia, the keystone of the action, he views with contemptuous regret as " 'a mere woman's whim.' " Hawthorne's final word on Westervelt would well fit Hovenden: "He was altogether earthly, worldly, made for time and its gross objects, and incapable—except by a sort of dim reflection caught from other minds—of so much as one spiritual idea."

Hovenden is also comparable, however, to more worthy characters. He has a tinge of the earthly honesty of "stout Silas Foster," the farmer of Blithedale, whose practicality is a good corrective of the soaring utopianism of the colonists. Like Westervelt, Foster is unable to perceive any but the grossest meaning, but his materialism takes a far more amiable form. Faced with the problem of the ethereal and mysterious Priscilla, whose enigma arouses in others the most romantic speculations, his estimate of her case within its limits is definitive: " 'give the girl a hot cup of tea, and a thick slice of this first-rate bacon,' said Silas, like a sensible man as he was. 'That's what she wants.' " The truth that man does not live by bread alone is beyond his understanding, but he thoroughly knows the truth that without bread man does not live at all. Hovenden, like Foster, possesses a certain solid virtue. So far as he sees what good is, he wishes Warland nothing but good. He loves his daughter even better than he loves his watch, and as grandfather he shares the real amenities of Robert Danforth's "fireside circle," from which the artist is forever exiled.

The materialism of the blacksmith Danforth is of a more innocent kind, although its effects upon Warland are almost equally destructive. Danforth has the sturdy integrity of a lower organism perfectly adjusted to its environment and immune from the ills, aberrations, and temptations of a higher and more delicate nature. The blacksmith had best be seen at his forge:

Within was seen the forge, now blazing up and illuminating the high and dusky roof, and now confining its lustre to a narrow precinct of the coal-strewn floor, according as the breath of the bellows was puffed forth or again inhaled into its vast leathern lungs. In the intervals of brightness it was easy to distinguish objects in remote corners of the shop and the horseshoes that hung upon the wall; in the momentary gloom the fire seemed to be glimmering amidst the vagueness of unenclosed space. Moving about in this red glare and alternate dusk was the figure of the blacksmith, well worthy to be viewed in so picturesque an aspect of light and shade, where the bright blaze struggled with the black night, as if each would have snatched his comely strength from the other. Anon he drew a white-hot bar of iron from the coals, laid it on the anvil, uplifted his arm of might, and was soon enveloped in the myriads of sparks which the strokes of his hammer scattered into the surrounding gloom.

"Now, that is a pleasant sight," said the old watchmaker. "I know what it is to work in gold; but give me the worker in iron after all is said and done. He spends his labor upon a reality."

Danforth is a "man of main strength," a "worker in iron." His physical force is pitted against the delicacy and physical weakness of Warland; the spiritual power of Warland thus implies a corresponding spiritual lack in the blacksmith, who is a kind of earth spirit and honest Vulcan, with the same incompleteness as is symbolized by the bodily defect of the Limping God. The dark-and-blazing imagery of his forge hints at once of hell-fire and of the warmth of the hearth, while in general the picture suggests the power, the spaciousness, and the mystery of a huge subterranean cavern containing unknown potentialities both for good and for evil. His shop is for Hawthorne the symbol of the heart, which we may call the unconscious, if we choose. Danforth is a creature of the bowels of the earth, in direct contrast to the artist, whose airy ethereality is fitly symbolized by the butterfly. Danforth represents the primitive power and centrality of the human spirit, Antaeus-like bound to the earth and susceptible neither to the glory nor to the danger of the soaring Warland. Superlatively central and safe, couched on the bedrock of actuality, he is one of the crowd, that great conservative in Hawthorne; one of the people of the heart. He dwells in the bosom of human society; his successful marriage to Annie is the logical consummation of his qualities, which might else be perverted to evil; and his domestic fireside, the counterpart of the forge, is the essence of social virtue. Warland, "seeking admittance to Danforth's fireside circle" (the artist, forever an outsider, can only visit), finds there "the man of iron, with his massive substance thoroughly warmed and attempered by domestic influences."

Danforth has many relatives in Hawthorne's pages, among them the earth-fiend Aminadab, the assistant of the scientist Aylmer, whose hoarse, chuckling laugh is to be heard exulting over the tragic failure of his master's aspirations. "Thus," says Hawthorne, "ever does the gross fatality of earth exult in its invariable triumph over the immortal essence. . . ." Another of these characters is the brutish Bartram, the lime-burner of "Ethan Brand," who is heavy earth set against the alienating fire of Brand's Unpardonable Sin. Here it is a question of extremes: the perverted heart against the perverse intellect, Bartram's brutality against the oversubtlety of Brand. Danforth is saved as these men are damned, for while he is capable of friendship and love, they are capable only of sullen rage or brutal mockery. They are exiled from society by their debasement as is Warland by his elevation. Danforth is far above them, as he is perhaps below Robert Hagburn, the foil to Septimius Felton, or Dr. Baglioni, the moral censor of Rappaccini.

Annie is a feminine and more refined Danforth, the embodiment of woman as social conservator, her unamiable common sense tempered and enlivened by a sensitivity which is tacitly understood to be feminine. The sympathy and the sisterly indulgence which she feels for Warland are mingled with a mocking contempt. She is, after all, Annie Hovenden in her origin. Danforth, not Warland, is her appropriate mate. She is one of that excellent and unexciting sisterhood in Hawthorne who might be called the watchers of the fireside, a species of faithful vestal matrons. This company is headed by Phoebe Pyncheon, the model of gentle domestic grace, the cultivated garden flower in whom all trace of wildness has been carefully bred out. Rose Garfield, the mate of Robert Hagburn in *Septimius Felton,* is also a close relation, as is the slightly drawn but most attractive Dorothy, the faithful wife in "The Gentle Boy." It is to be noticed of these women that, with all but the crowning virtues, they generally lack the final insight which would bring them fully to life. There is a kind of spiritual coarseness about them which makes them fail to do justice to a lofty nature. So Annie lets Warland down in the crisis; Rose Hagburn is unequal to Septimius Felton; and Phoebe Pyncheon is far from comprehending the depths of her lover Holgrave.

Hawthorne's intention clearly is to present Owen Warland as the spiritual norm of his tale and to proclaim through him the superior significance and intensity and the greater value of the artist's experience and interpretation of reality. As we have seen, however, Warland does not always show up well in his environment. This fact is a tribute to Hawthorne's imaginative honesty. The artist is in some degree Hawthorne himself, and therefore it is all the more necessary that he avoid manipulating the fictional truth in his favor. So, as is his custom, Hawthorne leans backward—at times a little too far backward. Although the parallel is not exact, his treatment of the artist may be compared to his treatment of the Puritans in *The Scarlet Letter* and "The Maypole of Merry

Mount." Himself Puritan in temperament, and possessed of a deep comprehension of the Puritan mind, he manhandles them unmercifully and yet with a certain affectionate familiarity. While Puritan, he is artist as well, and the Puritan in him is well able to take the world's part. The deprecation of Warland, consequently, comes from both sides of Hawthorne's nature—as Hawthorne portrays himself he deprecates, while as Puritan he reprehends with a "How shall the world be served?"

More important, however, is the Platonic fashion in which Hawthorne envisions the artist's gift. The notion of a transcendent reality is itself a paradox, for our imaginations fail to grasp it. Warland's physical smallness and his delicate minuteness of craftsmanship are intended to imply no lack of essential magnitude. His tiny butterfly transcends its spatial limitations; "In its perfect beauty, the consideration of size was entirely lost. Had its wings overreached the firmament, the mind could not have been more filled or satisfied." Undoubtedly the repeated emphasis upon Warland's physical smallness and weakness are meant to underline the opposition of ideal-material. What is true in the lower world is false in the higher; and Warland and his butterfly mock the pretensions of mere material bulk. But the imagination is at times inclined to prefer the lower truth, seeing with the eyes of a Hovenden or a Danforth. Faced with this paradox, Hawthorne does not attempt to solve it; rather, he dramatizes it. Danforth is superior to Warland as strength is to weakness, and he has the advantage of a sturdy masculinity. In a sense he is a greater artist. In the forge scene he is depicted as lifting from the fire a white-hot bar of iron, then shaping it with powerful strokes of the hammer. This is an image of creation, the molding of recalcitrant materials into unity, which calls to mind the mighty artist of Blake's "Tiger":

> *What the hammer? what the chain?*
> *In what furnace was thy brain?*
> *What the anvil? what dread grasp*
> *Dare its deadly terrors clasp?*

Blake, however, conceives a synthesis of strength and beauty which Hawthorne explicitly disavows, although he admits the hope of it as an ideal. The artist is disappointed in his faith that Annie is "imbued . . . with a finer grace, that might enable her to be the interpreter between strength and beauty."

The fact that Warland is a watchmaker lessens his dignity. The worker with mechanisms is soiled by the touch, even though he transforms his materials to living beauty. We cannot wholly forget the artisan in the artist. Warland is nearly unique in Hawthorne's work in that he successfully executes his ideal conception, and one cannot avoid considering that his success is partly due to the slightness of the archetype. He is unique in another respect: because of the peculiar nature of his art he runs no risk of violating the human heart, of losing the respect for the sanctity of the human spirit, as do those who imitate the human form or delve into human psychology. The painter of "The Prophetic Pictures" is one of the latter, as is Miles Coverdale, the "spiritualized Paul Pry" of *The Blithedale Romance*. It is perhaps significant that Hawthorne, in this his most extensive and explicit study of the problem of the artist, has exempted Warland from a danger with which he himself was undoubtedly preoccupied. In painting the ideal artist he has from

affection freed him from this temptation, left him un-
stained by "Earth's common lot of care and sorrow," and
in so doing weakened him.

Warland is isolated from society, as in Hawthorne
are all artists and indeed all men of extraordinary aspirations, capacity, or achievements. His isolation, however, is that of an unfallen nature in a fallen world, which
will not brook his pure pursuit of beauty, his urge for
freedom from the prison house of life. His isolation is
not self-inflicted but is forced upon him. From Annie he
seeks love, and through love to link himself with human
society, but his overtures are rejected. Love, the touching
of the heart, is itself a kind of Fall and is incompatible
with the attainment of the pure ideal. This fulfillment
in Warland would probably have precluded the fulfillment of art, and the resulting disillusion with actuality
might have achieved the same end as his final perception
of the meaning of the butterfly.

Had he become convinced of his mistake through the medium of successful love,—had he won Annie to his bosom,
and there beheld her fade from angel into ordinary woman,
—the disappointment might have driven him back, with con-
centrated energy, upon his sole remaining object. On the
other hand, had he found Annie what he fancied, his lot
would have been so rich in beauty that out of its mere redundancy he might have wrought the beautiful into many a
worthier type than he had toiled for. . . .

But neither of these alternatives occurs; one feels
that the possible choice is confined to an "either-or." Love
awakens to life, as Hawthorne proclaims in a famous letter; but it binds as well, as he suggests in the young lovers

of "The Maypole of Merry Mount." Love would be inappropriate to Warland, symbol of the free and soaring, whose triumph results from accepting his isolation and from perceiving the difference between the actual and the longed-for ideal. His wonderful butterfly, so pitilessly destroyed, is the scapegoat, the price of his freedom. It is the Warland of pure sensibility, Warland the seeker for sympathy and love, without the protective armor of knowledge which he himself has acquired painfully from conflict.

## VII

## *"Rappaccini's Daughter"*

I HAVE FOUND "Rappaccini's Daughter" the
most difficult of Hawthorne's stories. Upon
consideration, the difficulty seems to have two causes: the
symbolism of Beatrice Rappaccini is puzzling, and the
theme of the tale is double rather than single. "Rappaccini's Daughter" has, on the other hand, very great virtues; it is perhaps their very redundancy which makes
the story hard to interpret.

The first problem is the character of Beatrice Rappaccini. Beatrice is physically beautiful but deadly, her
scientist father having reared her from birth on poisons
which are through long habit harmless to herself but
destructive to anyone who should approach her closely.
Symbolically she should represent, then, a contrast between outward beauty and inner ugliness and evil. The
relation of physical to spiritual evil is made inescapable
by Hawthorne's reference to "those dreadful peculiarities
in her physical nature which could not be supposed to
exist without some corresponding monstrosity of soul."
Instead, however, she is essentially simple and good, her
evil power a mere superficial disguise. But the notion that
she is ineradicably and hopelessly evil is strengthened by
the effect of the draught administered by her lover Giovanni at the end of the story. This draught is supposed
to contain within it the very principle of good, but in-

stead of healing it kills her. "To Beatrice . . . as poison had been life, so the powerful antidote was death. . . ." Since in the story this potion represents the only hope of remedy, it seems unjust to her real goodness that she must die despite it; or else we must suppose, in contradiction to Hawthorne's plain statement and emphasis, that evil was predominant in her.

The second problem is the theme. Most interpretations of the story stress Rappaccini himself, the scientist who ignores all other values in his quest for knowledge and power. In reality, however, we see far more of Beatrice and of her lover, Giovanni Guasconti, particularly the latter, through whose eyes for the most part we see the action. This problem is more easily solved than the first. The real theme arises from Beatrice and Giovanni and concludes with a demonstration of Beatrice's spiritual superiority after both have undergone the severest possible trial. The theme of Rappaccini is secondary but encroaches upon the first from the importance and complexity of its issues. Consequently it is difficult to find a focus which will both enclose and clarify the picture of the entire story. In addition, Rappaccini's antagonist Dr. Baglioni also demands far more attention from the reader than his position would at first seem to require. "Rappaccini's Daughter," in fact, suffers from its excess of virtues; there are too many things to look at at once, and accurate definition of its elements is next to impossible.

Beatrice is exuberantly lovely, "beautiful as the day, and with a bloom so deep and vivid that one shade more would have been too much." She is luxuriant, "redundant with life, health, and energy." Yet like the gorgeous shrub which is her floral counterpart, she is wholly deadly to approach, "as terrible as she is beautiful." In the deepest truth of her nature, however, she is simple and good —"a simple, natural, most affectionate, and guileless creature." I have an explanation for this seeming confusion, though whether it solves it or merely describes it I must leave the reader to judge for himself. Hawthorne intends to tell of the greatest conceivable moral involvement which shall yet be consonant with the ultimate triumph of order and goodness. Beatrice dies saved, her soul untouched by the poisonous evil with which her earthly life has been so intimately entwined. But her human problem is almost or entirely insoluble. Confidence in absolute and eternal justice is placed in exact and dramatic opposition to human injustice and error.

The eternal, by which Beatrice is ultimately to be justified, is simple; the merely human, in which she sinks, is complex and confused. There are, however, two levels of simplicity in "Rappaccini's Daughter," one of which is inadequate to the task of just interpretation. This is "the light of common day," by which the puzzled Giovanni at times views the action before him, a light which "brought everything within the limits of ordinary experience." The simplicity of absolute truth is in Heaven, or Eden, where, as Beatrice says, " 'the evil which thou hast striven to mingle with my being will pass away like a dream.' " This Heaven is white light, or the transparent water of a "pure fountain." Such is the true nature of Beatrice, which the too-fallible Giovanni lacks insight to perceive.

The central symbols, Heaven and erring Earth, are the most prominent objects in the visual composition of Rappaccini's garden. The heaven symbol is the fountain in the center of the garden, "wofully shattered. . . . The water, however, continued to gush and sparkle into the sunbeams . . . as if the fountain were an immortal spirit that sung its song unceasingly and without heeding the vicissitudes around it. . . ." The fountain is the true and eternal Beatrice, unharmed by the evil of mortality. Near it stands the gorgeous but ominous shrub, splendid in purple—the symbol of the earthly Beatrice. Its glowing purple contrasts with the transparency of the fountain, its complex organism with the fountain's linear simplicity, its deadliness with the life-giving waters. The fountain is the inwardness of Beatrice's self, for "Her spirit gushed out like a fresh rill that was just catching its first glimpse of the sunlight." The shrub is the external Beatrice; Giovanni repeatedly notices "an analogy between the beautiful girl and the gorgeous shrub . . . a resemblance which Beatrice seemed to have indulged a fantastic humor in heightening, both by the arrangement of her dress and the selection of its hues."

It is Giovanni's error as well as Rappaccini's which precipitates the catastrophe of the story. Spectator and interpreter of a devious and complex reality, Giovanni alternately views it as simply matter-of-fact and as complexly evil but is incapable of perceiving its eternal aspect of simple good. Giovanni from his window looks down upon the fascinating tableau of the garden, where the ambiguous figures of Rappaccini and his daughter are walking. In daylight, from dawn to noon, he is "inclined to take a most rational view of the whole matter." It is different, however, "during the sun's decline, or among the shadows of the night, or in the less wholesome glow of moonshine." Then there are ominous signs that the garden and its dwellers are evil. A lizard dies at the touch of a drop of moisture from the giant shrub; a butterfly is killed by the mere proximity of Beatrice. In the clear sun of ordinary day Giovanni dismisses these incidents from his mind, but they cannot be forgotten. Hawthorne at this point suggests the choices open to the young man. The wisest, for himself, would be to "quit his lodgings and Padua itself at once." Next best would be to accustom himself "to the familiar and daylight view of Beatrice— thus bringing her rigidly and systematically within the limits of ordinary experience." Giovanni makes the mistake, however, of avoiding her sight while remaining close to her, a practice which awakens a morbid confusion of feeling.

Before further commenting on this confusion, it should be remarked that here Hawthorne fails by his symbolism to distinguish between the ordinary light of reason and common sense, "the familiar and daylight view of Beatrice," and the pure light which would lay bare her true goodness. For presumably the outward signs of evil, the deaths of the lizard and the butterfly, would have occurred in any light whatever; they are real and external events. The truest perception could not ignore them but would relegate them to their proper place in its final judgment. The unfortunate Giovanni is incapable of this highest insight and swings helplessly between a too-simple common sense, which sees only the beauty of Beatrice, and a morbid fear. The combination is disastrous.

Giovanni knew not what to dread; still less did he know what to hope; yet hope and dread kept a continual warfare in his breast, alternately vanquishing one another and starting up afresh to renew the contest. Blessed are all simple emotions, be they dark or bright! It is the lurid intermixture of the two that produces the illuminating blaze of the infernal regions.

This praise of simplicity has its problems. Naïve simplicity, or mere common sense, would hardly be enough to deal with this complex situation. The reader will probably consider that Giovanni knows too little rather than too much. The best simplicity will not seek to ignore what is actually present.

The "lurid intermixture" of Giovanni's emotions is the sign of his ruin. Instead of either mastering or escaping the difficulties, he yields to them, and is caught in the same web as Beatrice. His mind now mirrors the evil itself, which is expressed throughout the story in images of entanglement. Giovanni's mind is now the counterpart, like Beatrice, of the poisonous flowers, some of which are hybrid, "such commixture, and, as it were, adultery, of various vegetable species, that the production was no longer of God's making, but the monstrous offspring of man's depraved fancy. . . ." Beatrice's own enmeshment in evil is shown in the scene where she embraces the purple shrub and draws "its branches into an *intimate* embrace—so intimate that her features were hidden in its leafy bosom and her glistening ringlets all intermingled with the flowers." The flowers themselves are serpentine and insinuating in their profusion of growth: "some crept serpent-like along the ground or climbed on high, using whatever means of ascent was offered them. One plant had wreathed itself round a statue of Vertumnus, which was thus quite veiled and shrouded in a drapery of hanging foliage. . . ." Perhaps it is significant of a deeper damnation in Rappaccini that he avoids this influence: "there was no approach to inti-

macy between himself and these vegetable existences."
Giovanni, admitted at last into the garden, has to push
through "the entanglement of a shrub that wreathed its
tendrils over the hidden entrance. . . ."

Throughout "Rappaccini's Daughter" purple is the
color of complexity and evil, and white the color of goodness and simplicity. The complement of the glowing
purple is a rich perfume, made like the color of mingled
beauty and poison. Beatrice is repeatedly associated with
both; her voice makes Giovanni "think of deep hues of
purple or crimson and of perfumes heavily delectable."
The extent of Giovanni's entrapment is made obvious
when Dr. Baglioni notices a "faint, but delicious" perfume pervading his chamber. Both color and odor are
rich and sensuously alluring. It is noticeable that the underlying poison intermingles with the greatest physical
health and luxuriance. Beatrice "looked redundant with
life, health, and energy . . . in their luxuriance. . . ." The
flowers are profuse and gorgeous. Giovanni, unknowing-
ly infected at last with the poison, gazes in the mirror
to find that "his features had never before possessed so
rich a grace, nor his eyes such vivacity, nor his cheeks
so warm a hue of abundant life."

This contrast presents the same difficulty as the character of Beatrice herself and is susceptible of the same explanations, which may now be considered in detail. First,
as has earlier been remarked, the "intimate intermin-
gling" of glowing health with poison corresponds with
Hawthorne's intention of inventing the greatest possible
human dilemma. Second, it represents the same confusion
as the lack of distinction between the two levels of simplicity and has the same privative tendency. A fatality
attaches to creatures too richly endowed; Beatrice is *too*

beautiful, *too* perfect, like the flowers, and because of her very perfection she is marked for death. In this imperfect world she cannot long endure. It is not without relevance that Rappaccini has reared her, like the flowers, in an isolated garden, which is metaphorically associated with Eden. The world *must* break in, as it does in the person of Giovanni, with fatal results. It may be counted an instance of Rappaccini's spiritual blindness that he himself has believed it possible to expose his perfect creation to the world; in Giovanni he has planned to give his daughter a mate. Finally, the beauty of Beatrice and the gorgeous purple of the great shrub may be taken quite simply as good in themselves. Rappaccini is a great though impious creator; defying God, he has not wholly failed in his effort. Alternatively, the beauty of Beatrice is ultimately of God, who thus shows His mysterious providence. This interpretation might be borne out by the fact that the poisonous flowers are fed by the pure waters of the fountain, the emblem of eternity.

Beatrice and Giovanni are put to the same test. Beatrice conquers; Giovanni is lost. The poison in Beatrice is unable to touch her spirit, but Giovanni is wholly destroyed. The dying Beatrice asks, "Oh, was there not, from the first, more poison in thy nature than in mine?" Not that Giovanni is basically evil, unless all men are so. He enters the story a representative of us all, *l'homme moyen sensuel*. But he is ordinary and breaks beneath an extraordinary ordeal; Beatrice is exceptional.

So much for the primary theme of Beatrice and Giovanni. But more must be considered in "Rappaccini's Daughter." Rappaccini himself has generally occupied most attention, and naturally so, since in portraying him

Hawthorne has hit upon the most crucial contemporary issues. Since he has been well and fully discussed by others, we need not here attempt an exhaustive study. His character, however, leads into themes and motifs which must at least be mentioned.

Rappaccini is one of Hawthorne's scientific empirics, who are always at least partly evil but are also partly admirable. The best of them is perhaps Aylmer of "The Birthmark," and I do not think that Rappaccini is the worst. His sin is primarily in striving to rival God (so far as it is possible to man, since he cannot create but only alter God's creations), and secondarily in subordinating human values to scientific knowledge. Rappaccini is the God of an unnatural Paradise, his garden a perverted Eden. He is a false God, and is so proven at the conclusion, but his power in the interim is great. To some extent he governs the world of the story like a god and determines the action until the final catastrophe, when his plans are shattered. It is at least provisionally suggested that Giovanni from the beginning is in his toils; he has, of course, controlled the life of Beatrice. The Eden theme is continually suggested in the story, and in a tableau toward the end there is a parody of God in the Garden blessing the newly-created Adam and Eve:

As he drew near, the pale man of science seemed to gaze with a triumphant expression at the beautiful youth and maiden, as might an artist who should spend his life in achieving a picture or a group of statuary and finally be satisfied with his success. He paused; his bent form grew erect with conscious power; he spread out his hands over them in the attitude of a father imploring a blessing upon his children. . . .

Rappaccini, then, like Ethan Brand, is a daring rebel and blasphemer against God, a man of almost inconceivable presumption and pride. In spite of, or perhaps because of, his magnitude of evil, he is a figure of impressive dignity, a Lucifer. Hawthorne treats him with sympathy and at the end leaves us feeling a certain pity by showing us a tableau in which he is mocked by his enemy, the complacent Baglioni:

Just at that moment Professor Baglioni looked forth from the window, and called loudly, in a tone of triumph mixed with horror, to the thunder-stricken man of science,—

"Rappaccini! Rappaccini! and is *this* the upshot of your experiment!"

Here Rappaccini appears to better advantage than the virtuous Baglioni. With due regard for the difference in context, this scene suggests the malevolent laughter of the earth-demon Aminadab at the disaster of the aspiring Aylmer and the mockery of Hovenden at the Artist of the Beautiful. To put it more flatly, it is the revenge of the mediocre over the exceptional; to change the balance, it is in Hawthorne the victory of the heart over the head, an event with which we seldom feel wholly satisfied.

Any closer view, then, of the moral issues of "Rappaccini's Daughter" shows us a situation of great complexity. In any simple analysis of the story Rappaccini must be bad and Baglioni good, but consideration will lead us to modify, though not perhaps alter, our opinion. This point can be better explained by remarking that Hawthorne has taken the structure of Gothic romance, or Spenserian allegory, or better still fairy tale, and transformed it to mature art, with a very singular effect from

the juxtaposition of powerfully primitive fable with refined and subtle motivation.

From the Gothic romance the most significant element is the adaptation of the isolated castle as scene; in
"Rappaccini's Daughter" it becomes an old Italian palace with an enclosed garden. The most obvious effect is
an insulation from matter-of-fact reality, so that the story
occurs in a microcosm or realm of its own, governed by
its own laws. This, of course, is usual enough; we find
it in Poe, as in "The Fall of the House of Usher" or "Ligeia"; it is common in melodrama; and today we are
familiar with it in a thousand mystery novels. John
Dickson Carr, for example, makes skillful use of the
Gothic isolation to create atmosphere in the detective
story. In "Rappaccini's Daughter," however, it has a
serious and organic relation to meaning, for the palace
and garden are the enclosed domain of Rappaccini, whose
pretensions as ruler and creator are real.

Also Gothic is the figure of the heroine, who is beset
by mysterious and overpowering forces. In Hawthorne's
story, Giovanni rather than Beatrice fills this position,
since her fate has already been determined. Most important here is the sense of unequal struggle against tremendous odds which can be defeated only by some species
of miraculous intervention or by violation of the laws of
cause and effect. For in "Rappaccini's Daughter" it is
basic to the meaning that the intervention fails to come
off, the laws are not suspended, hero and heroine do not
escape. Much else in the story, for example Rappaccini
himself, might well be called Gothic; but it seems more
useful to point now to other associations. Rappaccini, as
Randall Stewart has noted, is related to the Archimago
and the Malbecco of *The Faerie Queene,* and Beatrice

and the garden to Acrasia in her Bower of Bliss and to Tasso's enchanting Armida. The value of such references lies, I think, in the richness of the ideas and emotions evoked by the comparison, which reveals above all an ironic reversal of terms. Giovanni is a pitiful Sir Guyon, or paladin of Charlemagne, and Beatrice is a sadly innocent and vulnerable sorceress. One further significant relation might be suggested: the story of Jason and Medea, in which the subtle enchantress is herself betrayed by the beautiful hero.

More basic still, perhaps, is the fairy tale, with the young prince and princess and a good and an evil fairy. Beatrice is thus the sleeping beauty, and Rappaccini is the malevolent fairy who has bewitched her. Baglioni is then the good fairy who tries to counteract the spell, and Giovanni is the handsome young prince who comes to her rescue. The powerful medicine of Baglioni is the magic potion which undoes the wrong. Something of the complex effect of "Rappaccini's Daughter" comes, then, from the elemental power and universal acceptability of the fairy tale motifs, developed and questioned as they are by Hawthorne. The handsome young prince—Giovanni is "a beautiful young man"—is an all-too-ordinary fellow, the evil enchanter is partially good, and the good fairy, Baglioni, is partially bad. The simple assumptions of the fairy tale, which we all instinctively accept, are ironically overturned. Hawthorne displays to us, not in mockery, the downfall of the heart's desire.

Not in mockery. The tone of "Rappaccini's Daughter" is elegiac. It mourns for the beauty of a past which never existed, save in imagination. "A young man, named Giovanni Guasconti, came, very long ago, from the more southern region of Italy, to pursue his studies at the University of Padua." It laments for the subversion of the heart's desire, for the lovely and perverted Eden of Rappaccini, and for the vanity of all human effort, even as it reasserts the fundamental justice of Providence. The tone is ironic without being cynical. "The young man rejoiced that, in the heart of the barren city, he had the privilege of overlooking this spot of lovely and luxuriant vegetation. It would serve, he said to himself, as a symbolic language to keep him in communion with Nature." And, in its delicate balance, a withdrawn quality which tempers the emotional sympathy also present, it never lapses into sentimentality.

# VIII

# "*My Kinsman, Major Molineux*"

"MY KINSMAN, MAJOR MOLINEUX" has in
recent years increased greatly in critical reputation. At least one critic has called it perhaps Hawthorne's most powerful short story, and it has been interpreted skilfully and at length. A chief reason for
its currency is undoubtedly the currency of psycho-
anthropological criticism: the situation of "My Kinsman,
Major Molineux" is archetypal, an initiation ceremony.
A country boy on the verge of maturity comes to the city
seeking his fortune through the favor of his influential
kinsman. He is confronted instead with the spectacle of
his relative tarred and feathered and carried in a cart
(like Captain Ireson) by the Boston mob, amid universal
laughter. Left with this reversal of his expectations, at
the end of the story he has presumably learned his lesson.
Hereafter he must depend upon himself.

"Major Molineux" has also been interpreted as an
allegory of New England history. The time is about
1730, the conflict is between the colonial governors and
the New England populace, an issue sharpened by the
withdrawal of the original charter of the people's lib-
erties. Major Molineux's power and wealth is associated
with the court party and the establishment, of which he
is a symbol, and his overthrow represents a triumph for
the rising democracy and nation. The hero, young Robin,

is dramatically forced to choose between the old and the new, the privileged or the people. (One may feel in this connection that Major Molineux is an unfortunate Colonel Pyncheon.)

Both interpretations are valid, and not incompatible. My own interest, however, does not lie wholly with either. As an illustration of an archetype the story is a little too universal; one would prefer if possible to see it more individually. As socio-historical allegory, on the other hand, it loses some of its juice. The historical situation is rather the base of operations than the total field of action, or perhaps the objective correlative of a wider meaning. The following explication will treat Robin more as folk-tale hero than as mythic hero or Freudian archetype, and will neither pass over nor emphasize his New England heritage. It may trespass a little on mythic grounds occasionally when the temptation is great.

"My Kinsman, Major Molineux" possesses the same clarity and centrality as does "Young Goodman Brown," though not quite the same ambiguity. Like the other tale it commences poised between day and night, and the hero passes into troubles of the night. As Goodman Brown enters the forest, Robin, "crossing alone the nighted ferry," enters Boston as it were over the River Styx. There is a touch of apt humor in the circumstance that instead of an obolus he pays the boatman with depreciated provincial currency; country values are at a discount in the city. Again, the maze of streets through which Robin wanders is like the winding forest path of Goodman Brown, a Spenserian Maze of Errour. The situations are likewise similar in dramatic irony, since each hero is struggling for knowledge amid almost insuperable difficulties. One would add that this irony has in each instance an element of pure fun, rather more extensive in "Molineux" than in "Young Goodman Brown."

Finally, the tales resemble each other at the point that raises "My Kinsman, Major Molineux" to greatness, the climax of each story. The Major, mocked and publicly humiliated, is a genuinely tragic figure, in what he represents and in himself. (It may be noted that his impact upon Robin is Aristotelian: "They stared at each other in silence, and Robin's knees shook, and his hair bristled, with a mixture of pity and terror.") As the procession resumes, "On they went, like fiends that throng in mockery around some dead potentate, mighty no more, but majestic still in his agony. On they went, in counterfeited pomp, in senseless uproar, in frenzied merriment, trampling all on an old man's heart." The final clause is the ultimate touch of imaginative insight. The immediate issue, however, is the passage's resemblance in rhetoric, tone, cadence, and feeling to the Devil's elegiac speech in "Young Goodman Brown": " 'Lo, there ye stand, my children,' said the figure, in a deep and solemn tone, almost sad with its despairing awfulness, as if his once angelic nature could yet mourn for our miserable race. 'Depending upon one another's hearts, ye had still hoped that virtue were not all a dream. Now are ye undeceived. Evil is the nature of mankind. Evil must be your only happiness. Welcome again, my children, to the communion of your race.' " The ambiguity involved in "My Kinsman, Major Molineux" is perhaps less deep, but it still rises from Hawthorne's fullest vision. The mockery of the Boston mob is justified and deep-rooted in its causes, but there is real substance in the object mocked.

"Molineux" has unusual humor and freshness, a

freshness more evident in the early than in the later tales of Hawthorne. It combines reserve with richness, with iron intellect and character reinforcing lightness of fancy, deepening to tragic imagination at its climax. Critics have properly noted the story's structural rhythm, which is more varied and subtle than most of them have supposed. Passing over the themes of wandering and nightmarish dream as all-pervasive, one observes three principal motifs: first, the insistent repetition of the fact that Robin is a "shrewd youth," along with his persistent aggressiveness; second, the recurrent laughter, which most critics have taken to be dominant; and, third, the continual influence of moonlight, an image insufficiently observed, and which I shall emphasize accordingly.

Robin's shrewdness is mentioned eight times, too often for accident. He is surprised at the rude laughter that greets his first inquiry after his kinsman, Major Molineux, "but, being a shrewd youth, soon thought himself able to account for the mystery." He makes various inferences, "with his usual shrewdness," about the meaning of his various encounters with townspeople. Most of these inferences are mistaken, but they are not lacking in ingenuity and resourcefulness. He is tempted by a pretty and inordinately hospitable girl, "But Robin, being of the household of a New England clergyman, was a good youth, as well as a shrewd one; so he resisted temptation, and fled away." Startled by the fantastic disguise of a man he had seen earlier in a different aspect, he consumes a few moments "in philosophical speculations upon the species of man who had just left him; but having settled this point shrewdly, rationally, and satisfactorily, he was compelled to look elsewhere for his amusement." Explaining himself to a friendly stranger, the only *friendly* stranger he meets, he remarks that "I have the name of being a shrewd youth"; to be answered good-naturedly, "I doubt not you deserve it." Shocked and disenchanted, at the end of the story Robin asks his new friend the way to the ferry, to which the gentleman replies, "if you prefer to remain with us, perhaps as you are a shrewd youth, you may rise in the world without the help of your kinsman, Major Molineux."

Now, what of this shrewdness? Daniel G. Hoffman *(Form and Fable in American Fiction)* remarks that "There are buffetings of passion, there are possibilities of evil and of guilt, which Robin's callow rationalism cannot fathom." Robin is the Yankee Bumpkin, and "Like his antecedent bumpkins in popular tradition—Brother Jonathan, the peddlers of folk anecdote, Jack Downing, Sam Slick—he is nothing if not shrewd. But Robin is shrewd only by his own report." Mr. Hoffman concludes that "Robin, the shrewd youth from the backwoods, proves to be the Great American Boob, the naif whose odyssey leads him, all uncomprehending, into the dark center of experience." One can agree with this assessment of Robin as with very much else in Hoffman's good essay on "Molineux," and still feel that there is another side to the question.

Robin, that is, is the young hero of folk and fairy tale, transplanted in a higher genre of story. In this he is like Giovanni and Beatrice of "Rappaccini's Daughter," the lovely maiden and the fairy prince exposed to sad reality, yet treated with affection, not wholly extricated from their charming original setting. Robin is the younger brother who sets out to seek his fortune ("The elder brother was destined to succeed to the farm which his father cultivated in the interval of sacred duties; it was therefore determined that Robin should profit by his kinsman's generous intentions, especially as he seemed to be rather the favorite, and was thought to possess other necessary endowments"). The irony is of course, as Mr. Hoffman suggests, that this shrewd, courageous, attractive youth is quite inadequate to the situation he encounters, and that his shrewdness and courage and self-assurance turn against him.

His qualities and defects, however, are those of youth, which we commonly accept and even approve as such, considering them fair promises for the man to come. Robin's aggressiveness is as evident as his "shrewdness"; he carries "a heavy cudgel formed of an oak sapling," which he is unduly ready to use. "Oh," says he, "if I had one of those grinning rascals in the woods, where I and my oak sapling grew up together, I would teach him that my arm is heavy though my purse is light!" Unquestionably his combativeness is close to ludicrous. Yet Robin is a young, proud boy, who is suffering unexpected and sudden humiliations for unknown causes. His resentment is forgivable; and it would seem to be axiomatic that in a story of growth and maturity we should not blame the hero overmuch for being immature. Robin, in short, is essentially sound. His shrewdness and his goodness are genuine; if they are not, indeed, the story loses in intensity and complexity. Which is by no means to say that Hawthorne accepts him as the norm; rather, that he portrays him with humor and good nature, a Yankee Theseus or Hercules whose talents do not fit his predicament, but who turns out in the end to be laudably adaptable.

Laughter in "My Kinsman, Major Molineux" stands primarily for discord and disharmony. As Hawthorne said later in "Ethan Brand," "Laughter, when out of place, mistimed, or bursting forth from a disordered state of feeling, may be the most terrible modulation of the human voice. The laughter of one asleep, even if it be a little child—the madman's laugh—the wild, screaming laugh of a born idiot—are sounds that we sometimes tremble to hear, and would always willingly forget. Poets have imagined no utterance of fiends or hobgoblins so fearfully appropriate as a laugh." The laughter in "Molineux" is often mocking and sometimes fiendish. In his first encounter Robin is "pursued by an ill-mannered roar of laughter from the barber's shop." A little later he is driven from the public-room of a tavern amid "a general laugh, in which the inn-keeper's voice might be distinguished, like the dropping of small stones into a kettle." Next, enquiring for his kinsman of a watchman, he is dismissed to the sound of "drowsy laughter," echoed by "a pleasant titter" from "the lady of the scarlet petticoat" who tries to lure him within.

The approach of the procession escorting the unfortunate Molineux is heralded by "a wild and confused laughter," which continues at intervals until the cart with his kinsman in it is halted right before Robin's horrified eyes. The boy's first response is the pity and terror earlier mentioned, but soon "a bewildering excitement began to seize upon his mind . . . a perception of tremendous ridicule in the whole scene affected him with a sort of mental inebriety." And at this moment the laughter of the night is re-echoed and recapitulated: "a voice of sluggish merriment" from the watchman, "a peal of laughter like the ringing of silvery bells" from the lady of the scarlet petticoat, "A sharp, dry cachinnation" from the innkeeper. Finally there is "a great, broad laugh" from a dignified and pompous old citizen who had repelled Robin earlier in the evening with the rest.

It will be noticed that this laughter is modulated and varied. It begins in mockery, but it is no longer wholly unfriendly, and there is an element of fun in it, of sheer enjoyment of the situation. Not forgetting the tragedy —for later the procession sweeps on "in senseless uproar, in frenzied merriment, trampling all on an old man's heart"—it ends in being therapeutic, substituting a catharsis of comedy for that of tragedy. At the culminating laugh of the old citizen "Robin seemed to hear the voices of the barbers, of the guests of the inn, and of all who had made sport of him that night. The contagion was spreading among the multitude, when all at once, it seized upon Robin, and he sent forth a shout of laughter that echoed through the street,—every man shook his sides, every man emptied his lungs, but Robin's shout was the loudest there. The cloud-spirits peeped from their silvery islands, as the congregated mirth went roaring up the sky! The Man in the Moon heard the far bellow. 'Oho,' quoth he, 'the old earth is frolicsome to-night!' "

"Frolicsome," one observes. The laughter in "My Kinsman, Major Molineux," commences as discord and apparently cruel mockery, but expands until it becomes cosmic, impersonal, an exquisite lighthearted critique of man himself and perhaps his maker too. The cruelty of it does not wholly vanish, but is sublimated and spiritualized. Robin, caught up with it, laughs at himself and inevitably at his poor kinsman. Undergoing a reaction that is both emotional and intellectual, he is shaken, purged, emptied, and cleansed.

The reference to the listening Man in the Moon

seems almost childishly fanciful, but is imaginative and organic as well, for moonlight plays a very large part indeed in "Molineux"; the action of it is, in Wallace Stevens' words, "Panic in the face of the moon" in the old root meaning of "panic." As in Coleridge and Keats, moonlight is for Hawthorne a symbol of imagination, and at one point in the story he says in words that might have come from Coleridge that "the moon, creating, like the imaginative power, a beautiful strangeness in familiar objects, gave something of romance to a scene that might not have possessed it in the light of day." Hawthorne accepted, as I think, Coleridge's famous definitions of the imagination and the fancy, but in practice he was little concerned to observe Coleridge's careful distinctions between them; nor did he ever wholly accede to the Romantic idea of Keats that "What the imagination seizes as beauty must be truth." In "My Kinsman, Major Molineux" imagination and fancy are merged in the moonlight, which provides aesthetic distance and artifice along with complexity and depth of reality; feeling along with heartlessness; and sympathy together with steady detachment.

For Hawthorne moonlight is a specialized and aesthetic vision, deep but not always trustworthy, selective in emphasis, sometimes warm with sympathy but more frequently cold. One lives beneath the moon at moments only; Robin's experience in moonlit Boston is unique for him. In a sense it is the nightmare of a man who sleeps exposed to the moon's influence, a kind of lunacy. What happens in "My Kinsman, Major Molineux" constitutes the events of a night, and perhaps of a very special night, as in *A Midsummer Night's Dream*, where the characters act under the influence of enchantment. One remarks that Hawthorne's night-watchman, "like the Moonshine of Pyramus and Thisbe, carried a lantern, needlessly aiding his sister luminary in the heavens."

Nevertheless, unreality at one level can hide a deeper reality, and unusual circumstances reveal representative feelings. The moon is beauty and decorative design in the story; it isolates and distances, it is the atmosphere, like the castle of a Gothic romance or Poe's "Ligeia," it is a luminous ambiguity; but in it is the verity of buried consciousness. It functions, too, as my colleague Richard Adams has suggested to me, to alienate Robin as a necessary part of his transformation and development. In order that he may see clearly what and where he is, he must first be drawn apart from his surroundings.

The tale commences "near nine o'clock of a moonlight evening," and the ferryman who is to convey Robin to Boston "lifted a lantern, by the aid of which, and the newly risen moon, he took a very accurate survey of the stranger's figure." Searching for his kinsman through the streets of Boston, Robin notes an old house, "where the moonlight enters at the broken casement." He wanders by the water-side, where "the masts of vessels pierced the moonlight above the tops of the buildings." A little later "The light of the moon, and the lamps from the numerous shop-windows, discovered people promenading on the pavement, and amongst them Robin hoped to recognize his hitherto inscrutable relative." (Incidentally, Robin's wanderings must have been remarkably swift. At this moment "the ringing of a bell announced the hour of nine," whereas the ferryman picked up Robin at the outset "near nine o'clock.")

Approaching a half-opened door, "All that Robin

could discern was a strip of scarlet petticoat, and the occasional sparkle of an eye, as if the moonbeams were trembling on some bright thing." At Robin's appeal "the female, seeing nothing to be shunned in the handsome country youth, thrust open the door, and came forth into the moonlight." The lady of the petticoat suggests one of the less reputable moon-goddesses of mythology, a déclassée Astarte: "her bright eyes possessed a sly freedom," and even her voice is moonlike, "the airy counterpart of a stream of melted silver." There may be some point in adding, in connection with the moon's influence, that her bright eyes "triumphed over those of Robin."

Presently Robin comes upon a church, the rendezvous where he has been promised he will encounter his kinsman. Here moonlight plays its part most fully and subtly.

Then he strove to speed away the time, by listening to a murmur which swept continually along the street, yet was scarcely audible, except to an unaccustomed ear like his; it was a low, dull, dreamy sound, compounded of many noises, each of which was at too great a distance to be separately heard. Robin marvelled at this snore of a sleeping town, and marvelled more whenever its continuity was broken by now and then a distant shout, apparently loud where it originated. But altogether it was a sleep-inspiring sound, and, to shake off its drowsy influence, Robin arose, and climbed a window-frame, that he might view the interior of the church. There the moonbeams came trembling in, and fell down upon the deserted pews, and extended along the quiet aisles. A fainter yet more awful radiance was hovering around the pulpit, and one solitary ray had dared to rest upon the open page of the great Bible. Had nature, in that deep hour, become a worshipper in the house which man had builded? Or was that heavenly light the visible sanctity of the place,—visible because no earthly and impure feet were within the walls? The scene made Robin's heart shiver with a sensation of loneliness stronger than he had ever felt in the remotest depths of his native woods; so he turned away and sat down again before the door.

Sleep and dream pave the way for visionary imagination, while ironically and unknown to Robin the "low, dull, dreamy sound" is the roar of the crowd that is witnessing his kinsman's ritual humiliation. The effect upon Robin is like the hypnotic effect of the "Ode to a Nightingale"—"My heart aches, and a drowsy numbness pains/ My sense, as though of hemlock I had drunk." It isolates him, it bares him to receive the revelation of light. Yet the moonlight isolates him and alienates him still further, though it is heavenly, for its "visible sanctity" depends upon a lonely and an inhuman purity. Naturally it is lonelier than "the remotest depths of his native woods," for solitude is proper to these, while the church is made for congregation. It is the unaccustomed amid the usual and familiar that shocks to imagination. Robin, too, is the more desolate because of the church's association with his past, both in sameness and difference, a familiar and reverenced object set in a context that is strange to him.

These associations carry him back to the past that he has lost, his father at "domestic worship" under a great oak at evening, with his family and friends about him. Again with some irony, Robin carries a reminder of this in his oak cudgel, which retains "a part of the hardened root" as a sign of his and its origins. But his father holds the Scriptures not in the moon's cold rays, but "in the golden light" of the setting sun, benedictory though it may be premonitory too: the sun, that calls not to solitude but to assembly. "Am I here, or there?" cries Robin, suddenly starting (a question not unlike Keats's, "Fled is that music; do I wake or sleep?"). And in the moonlight, though now "the long, wide, solitary street shone out before him," "still his mind kept vibrating between fancy and reality; by turns, the pillars of the balcony lengthened into the tall, bare stems of pines, dwindled down to human figures, settled again into their true shape and size, and then commenced a new succession of changes." This is the vision's dramatic aftermath, buttressed as it were in moonlight by wavering pillars. More deeply, too, it images Robin's crisis of past and present, of childhood and maturity in balance, as the pines and pillars alternate before his moonlit eyes. He is undergoing an experience at once rare and universal, that is illuminated by the special light of imagination and art.

## IX

# *"The Birthmark"*

IT IS STRANGE but natural that "The Birthmark" should combine an explicit moral with
some of Hawthorne's densest ambiguities. If this sounds
strange but unnatural, one may reflect that, in Coleridge's
words, "Extremes meet"; that is, a strong impulse in one
direction evokes an equally strong opposite impulse in
reaction to it. Or it may be a question of Hawthorne's
artistic judgment, which perceives a need for enriching
bareness and abstraction with the compensations of complexity.

The moral is adumbrated at the beginning of the
story and stated at the end. Aylmer, a dedicated scientist,
marries the beautiful Georgiana, with consequent complications. "Such a union took place, and was attended
with truly remarkable consequences and a deeply impressive moral." Georgiana is physically perfect except
for a birthmark on her cheek. Aylmer, a passionate per-
fectionist, tries to eradicate it; he succeeds, but as with
Beatrice Rappaccini it is at the cost of Georgiana's life.
The story concludes, "Yet, had Aylmer reached a profounder wisdom, he need not thus have flung away the
happiness which would have woven his mortal life of the
selfsame texture with the celestial. The momentary circumstance was too strong for him; he failed to look beyond the shadowy scope of time, and, living once for

all in eternity, to find the perfect future in the past." The proposition is quite clear: Aylmer, to state the case moderately, has made a serious mistake.

Yet Hawthorne's attitude is so removed and imperturbable that nothing in the story can be taken simply; in "The Birthmark" he reaches his furthest range of disengagement. The point of view is so detached that his irony is frequently universalized and objectified into humor, and as in "My Kinsman, Major Molineux" the action is a consummate joke upon the principal actors. There is an airy levity, for instance, in the observation that Aylmer "had left his laboratory to the care of an assistant, cleared his fine countenance from the furnace smoke, washed the stain of acids from his fingers, and persuaded a beautiful woman to become his wife." Hawthorne's humor has been little investigated, it may be from its delicacy, and Anthony Trollope's penetrating comment on the humor of *The Scarlet Letter* has never been adequately pursued:

But through all this intensity of suffering, through this blackness of narrative, there is ever running a vein of drollery. As Hawthorne himself says, "a lively sense of the humorous again stole in among the solemn phantoms of her thought." He is always laughing at something with his weird, mocking spirit. The very children when they see Hester in the streets are supposed to speak of her in this wise: "Behold, verily, there is the woman of the scarlet letter. Come, therefore, and let us fling mud at her." Of some religious book he says, "It must have been a work of vast ability in the somniferous school of literature." "We must not always talk in the market-place of what happens to us in the forest," says even the sad mother to her child. Through it all there is a touch of burlesque,—not as to the suffering of the sufferers, but as to the great question whether it signifies much in what way we suffer, whether by crushing sorrows or little stings. Who would not sooner be Prometheus than a yesterday's tipsy man with this morning's sick-headache? In this way Hawthorne seems to ridicule the very woes which he expends himself in depicting.

Trollope, in true nineteenth-century fashion, is puzzled and amused by Hawthorne's gloom, for which he sees little occasion in reality. Hawthorne's humor is therefore all the more piquant to him from the shock of finding it; and it is, one may add, omnipresent in his fiction. *The Scarlet Letter,* as Trollope sees, is the most interesting instance of his humor because of the intensity and lack of relief of the book in its total effect.

We have spoken of the detachment of Hawthorne's attitude. Humor, however, traditionally involves sympathy, and Hawthorne shows a great deal of sympathy for his hero Aylmer. As Cleanth Brooks and Robert Penn Warren have remarked in *Understanding Fiction,* "The author is sympathetic to him, and obviously sees in his ruinous experiment a certain nobility." Again it is a case of Coleridge's meeting of extremes. As I have used these terms, irony in Hawthorne is lifted and objectified into humor, since irony contains a certain animus that interferes with objectivity, while humor sees the whole steadily and to a degree affectionately. Hawthorne's attitude and "tone" are then subtly varied and complex, and nowhere are more so than in "The Birthmark."

Aylmer is shown to be wrong, no doubt of it; but Aylmer is given a remarkably good run for his money. If he hangs himself, Hawthorne gives him a very long rope. The author is more engaged in his Faustian quest for knowledge and his Romantic pursuit of infinite development than most critics have seen, since the keenest critics of the story have usually been anti-Romantic. That at the last he can disengage himself is the more notable because of his sympathy with Aylmer.

This stress between detachment and sympathy renders "The Birthmark" one of Hawthorne's most intellectually lively tales, and with its richness of texture one of his best. It comes close to Poe in searching out abnormal experience and phenomena for their own sakes, for the wonders of Aylmer's laboratory resemble the perverse music and art with which Roderick Usher surrounds himself. This element of wondrous perversity is worth examining at some length. Its presence in the story is supported by one of Hawthorne's sources for it, as recorded in his *American Notebooks* in 1842, the approximate date of the story (1843). He cites

the case quoted in Combe's Physiology from Pinel, of a young man of great talents and profound knowledge of chemistry, who had in view some new discovery of importance. In order to put his mind into the highest possible activity, he shut himself up, for several successive days, and used various methods of excitement; he had a singing girl with him; he drank spirits; smelled penetrating odors, sprinkled cologne-water around the room &c &c. Eight days thus passed, when he was seized with a fit of frenzy, which terminated in a mania.

In "The Birthmark" the various stimuli act upon Georgiana, not Aylmer, who is in fact their source. They are a means both of amusing her and of preparing her mentally and physically for the change she must undergo. "Georgiana . . . found herself breathing an atmosphere of penetrating fragrance, the gentle potency of which had recalled her from her deathlike faintness. The scene around her looked like enchantment." Aylmer has converted the "smoky, dingy, sombre rooms" of his customary laboratory into chambers of fantasy, in which gorgeous curtains, "concealing all angles and straight lines, appeared to shut in the scene from infinite space. For aught Georgiana knew, it might be a pavilion among the clouds." Significantly Aylmer, excluding the natural sunlight "which would have interfered with his chemical processes, had supplied its place with perfumed lamps, emitting flames of various hue, but all uniting in a soft, impurpled radiance."

To sooth and distract Georgiana's mind, Aylmer calls upon his scientific skill to surround her with wonders. "Airy figures, absolutely bodiless ideas, and forms of unsubstantial beauty came and danced before her, imprinting their momentary footsteps on beams of light." The illusion of these "was almost perfect enough to warrant the belief that her husband possessed sway over the spiritual world." When she wishes to look out, "immediately, as if her thoughts were answered, the procession of external existence flitted across a screen." (Here one is inclined to suspect that Aylmer has invented television, and to wish him damned accordingly and forthwith. But there is an escape for him; his scenes are painted rather than photographed, imitations rather than copies of reality. "The scenery and the figures of actual life were perfectly represented, but with that bewitching, yet indescribable difference which always makes a picture, an image, or a shadow so much more attractive than the original.") Next Aylmer produces a flower of miraculously swift growth, and bids his wife pluck it. "But Georgiana had no sooner touched the flower than the whole plant suffered a blight, its leaves turning coal-black as if by the agency of fire. 'There was too powerful a stimulus,' said Aylmer thoughtfully."

Later he tries to take Georgiana's portrait "by a scientific process of his own invention," which involves "rays of light striking upon a polished plate of metal." The result is "blurred and indefinable; while the minute figure of a hand appeared where the cheek should have been." As the experiment goes on, he speaks to her of the elixir of life, which is within his option to perfect; shows her a small vial containing a perfume "capable of impregnating all the breezes that blow across a kingdom"; and finally exhibits to her "a gold-colored liquor" that is "the most precious poison that ever was concocted in this world," in a small crystal globe. During this time Georgiana begins "to conjecture that she was already subjected to certain physical influences, either breathed in with the fragrant air or taken with her food. She fancied likewise, but it might be altogether fancy, that there was a stirring up of her system—a strange, indefinite sensation creeping through her veins, and tingling, half painfully, half pleasurably, at her heart." Failing to eradicate the birthmark by all lesser methods, Aylmer finally concocts "a liquor colorless as water, but bright enough to be the draught of immortality." It turns out to be so indeed, since it eliminates first "the birthmark of mortality" and shortly afterward Georgiana herself—presumably to Aylmer's consternation, though this too remains ambiguous.

This account is perverse insofar as it explores extreme and unnatural experience for its own sake, as Poe explores the abnormal sensations of the hypersensitive Roderick Usher. The perversity of it shades off into the pleasure of aesthetic contemplation: the chambers, golden liquids, crystal globes, and the like, are presented to us as beautiful. Thus far Hawthorne indulges in a kind of Romanticism that should not be ignored in him. One must add, of course, a meaning and morality quite different from Poe's. Most obvious is the suggestion of illusion: everything that Aylmer has created is false and unnatural, like the gorgeous flowers of Rappaccini's garden. The light is artificial, the figures are shadows, the plant dies at the touch of reality, and the draught of immortality is the draught of death. The images all reflect Aylmer's spirituality, emphasized throughout the story; and this spirituality of his is spurious.

Under the beautiful illusion he has evoked is the grim bareness of his reality, which Georgiana at length penetrates in his laboratory.

The first thing that struck her eye was the furnace, that hot and feverish worker, with the intense glow of its fire, which by the quantities of soot clustered above it seemed to have been burning for ages. There was a distilling apparatus in full operation. Around the room were retorts, tubes, cylinders, crucibles, and other apparatus of chemical research. An electrical machine stood ready for immediate use. The atmosphere felt oppressively close, and was tainted with gaseous odors which had been tormented forth by the processes of science. The severe and homely simplicity of the apartment, with its naked walls and brick pavement, looked strange, accustomed as Georgiana had become to the fantastic elegance of her boudoir.

This scene evokes, like Melville's chapter on "The Whiteness of the Whale," John Locke's famous doctrine of secondary attributes in the perception, in which we ourselves attribute color, form, and life itself to a world intrinsically blank and unknowable. The doctrine underlies Addison's *Spectator* essays on "The Pleasures of Imagination," and the fact is relevant, for Locke's theory makes Addison's "imagination" a lovely and charming illusion, and the world a painted charnel house. Now, Aylmer is figuratively an artist and a practitioner of the imagination, who has created an artistic world for his beloved to dwell in; but it is false.

Something remains to be said of the reality, as also of what has so far been treated as illusion. Our first impression of the laboratory is simply its matter-of-fact bareness. Yet the furnace has a diabolic air, like the lime-kiln of "Ethan Brand," and the circumstance that its sootiness makes it seem "to have been burning for ages" reminds us of the blackened prison of *The Scarlet Letter*, the emblem of time, sin, and death. More favorably, too, it is the furnace of the human heart, like Robert Danforth's smithy, or the huge central chimney that is the heart of the house of the seven gables. Its reality is more than a bare negation.

There is also another side to be presented of Aylmer's creativity. The chambers and the laboratory are the image of his mind and moral being, and here lies a deep ambiguity. What if artistic illusion be awarded a reality of its own? Aylmer is an idealist in pursuit of the infinite, and the scene he has created appears to be shut in "from infinite space." "For aught Georgiana knew, it might be a pavilion among the clouds." To say too suddenly that his illusion is delusion is to ignore an important and an evident portion of Hawthorne's sensibility, which delights like Shelley's in paradoxes of airy form and insubstantial solidity. "Its wheels are solid clouds," says Shelley *(Prometheus Unbound)* of his Earth-Child's chariot, and Hawthorne would have approved the figure. Georgiana's chambers suggest his "Hall of Fantasy," which admits "the light of heaven only through stained and pictured glass, thus filling the hall with many-colored radiance . . . so that its inmates breathe, as it were, a visionary atmosphere . . . ." This hall substitutes like the chambers of Georgiana, a "purple atmosphere for unsophisticated sunshine." It is not to be lived in always or by everyone, but it is the appropriate residence of the artist. Of it is remarked on the one hand that "the fantasies of one day are the deepest realities of a future one," and on the other that "The white sunshine of actual life is necessary in order to test them."

One repeats that Hawthorne's sensibility has its Shelleyan side, and that the affinity is more than superficial. In "Earth's Holocaust" he singles him out: "methought Shelley's poetry emitted a purer light than almost any other productions of his day." To document more generally the light of imagination, one might also adduce the north light of the artist, as Miriam explains its necessity to Donatello in *The Marble Faun* when he visits her studio. One cannot, in fact, deny to the imagination a provisional reality and value, a place (to speak advisedly) in the sun; and Aylmer is imaginative artist as well as scientist.

From still another angle the situation is less favorable to him. Georgiana's regimen, with its gradually increasing steps of unseen and dimly felt influence, represents one of Hawthorne's portrayals of an entrapment.

It is most like the insidious process by which Dr. Rappaccini entangles Giovanni Guasconti, although less elaborate; it resembles the subtle temptation of Goodman Brown by the Devil; and Georgiana's sensations are similar to the Reverend Mr. Dimmesdale's while he is being mentally tortured by the unsuspected Chillingworth. Aylmer's purposes are less insane than Rappaccini's, and unlike the Devil and Chillingworth he seeks his patient's or victim's good. His policy is no worse than a well-meaning physician's, who confides to his patient only a part of his method of treatment. Nevertheless there is an ugly element of concealment and perfidy in it, and we feel that Aylmer tries to play God and succeeds in playing the devil instead. Thus there are continual ironies from his misconceptions, as when, after talking of his powers, he bids Georgiana "consider how trifling, in comparison, is the skill requisite to remove this little hand [the birthmark]." He does not, as Robert Heilman says confusing the symbol with the reality, comprehend that in trying to change her he is undertaking incomparably the most difficult as well as the most impious task of all.

Aylmer is artist, idealist, God, and unwitting devil; and as Heilman maintains in his classic essay "Hawthorne's 'The Birthmark': Science as Religion," he is scientist-priest as well. Heilman notes that science and religion are interchangeable in the story, both in Aylmer's terms and the terms that are used to describe him. One might comment, too, that as scientist (and of course as artist) Aylmer plays the role of wizard.

Both Aylmer's gifts and his aspirations approach to wizardry. The story is set at a time when "the comparatively recent discovery of electricity and other kindred mysteries of Nature seemed to open paths into the region of miracle," although it is also, we must note, specified that "We know not whether Aylmer possessed this degree of faith in man's ultimate control over Nature." Watching over his wife, he is confident "that he could draw a magic circle round her within which no evil might intrude." Of his swift-growing plant Georgiana explains, "It is magical!" In his aspirations he cites the alchemists; and his wife says fearfully that "It is terrible to possess such power, or even to dream of possessing it." In his library are "the works of the philosophers of the middle ages, such as Albertus Magnus, Cornelius Agrippa, Paracelsus, and the famous friar who created the prophetic Brazen Head."

Hawthorne's conception of science has generally been considered rather comically old-fashioned, but with the growth of the twentieth century the joke would seem to have turned against his critics. For most of us the chemist, the nuclear physicist, and the biologist are indeed wizards, and the disproportion between scientific and humanist advances in knowledge has become a commonplace, as has the power of scientism. Aylmer's claims seem less striking when one considers current progress in creating life, in indefinitely prolonging it, and of course in exploring and mastering space, motion, and matter itself. With this power, too, inevitably comes the claim, not necessarily from the scientist, that it is all-sufficient. Thus Heilman says of Aylmer that "His tragedy is that he lacks the tragic sense; he is, we may say, a characteristic modern, the exponent of an age which has deified science and regards it as an irresistibly utopianizing force. His tragic flaw is to fail to see the tragic flaw in humanity." "The Birthmark," in short,

127

raises vital and explosively timely issues, and Aylmer represents the claims of modern scientism.

He is not, however, only a scientist, as has already been shown at length. He is also a Romantic and transcendental artist, holding like Owen Warland, the artist of the beautiful, Platonic conceptions of reality in form and idea. Aylmer does not, like Warland, catch "a better butterfly than this," or if he does it is with a supreme and Aristotelian irony of reversal; and Warland does not, like Aylmer, trifle with a human being. Nor so far as we can tell does Aylmer achieve self-knowledge as does the Artist; instead, as with Giovanni Guasconti the conclusion leaves him high and dry. Still, as I have said, Hawthorne gives him a very long rope, as artist, as thinker, and as man.

Among the several notebook memoranda for the story is "A person to be the death of his beloved in trying to raise her to more than mortal perfection; yet this should be a comfort to him for having aimed so highly and holily" (1839). Here the balance is remarkably even, and *holily* cannot be passed over. Aylmer is, as Heilman brands him, "a romantic perfectibilitarian, who suffers from a dangerous fastidiousness in the presence of complex actuality," but perhaps Heilman feels a little worse about this than Hawthorne did. Aylmer's distaste for the birthmark arises from an aesthetic and moral sense of disharmony in it. "Had she been less beautiful, —if Envy's self could have found aught else to sneer at, —he might have felt his affection heightened by the prettiness of this mimic hand . . . but seeing her otherwise so perfect, he found this one defect grow more and more intolerable with every moment of their united

128

Greek
myth.

lives." He sets out to remove the flaw in the spirit of Pygmalion.

Aylmer's purposes are controlled by morality. Whereas Rappaccini "would sacrifice human life, his own among the rest, or whatever else was dearest to him, for the sake of adding so much as a grain of mustard seed to the great heap of his accumulated knowledge," there are some experiments that Aylmer will not undertake. He believes, for example, that the *elixir vitae* lies within his grasp, but does not attempt it, since he also believes "that it would produce a discord in Nature which all the world, and chiefly the quaffer of the immortal nostrum, would find cause to curse." Again, he possesses "the most precious poison that ever was concocted in this world. By its aid I could apportion the lifetime of any mortal at whom you might point your finger." He does not intend to use it thus, however: "its virtuous potency is yet greater than its harmful one."

Aylmer's notebook, which Georgiana comes upon, expounds his case most sympathetically and fully. In it he has recorded every experiment of his scientific career. "The book, in truth, was both the history and emblem of his ardent, ambitious, imaginative, yet practical and laborious life. He handled physical details as if there were nothing beyond them; yet spiritualized them all, and redeemed himself from materialism by his strong and eager aspiration towards the infinite. In his grasp the veriest clod of earth assumed a soul." Georgiana concludes her reading with a love and reverence more profound than ever for her husband, but a lesser confidence in his judgment. "Much as he had accomplished, she could not but observe that his most splendid successes were almost invariably failures, if compared with the ideal at which he aimed." One might appeal to *The Marble Faun* to denominate this praise, recalling how the novel prefers the rough sketch of the artist to the finished picture. Aylmer's volume is "the sad confession and continued exemplification of the shortcomings of the composite man, the spirit burdened with clay and working in matter, and of the despair that assails the higher nature at finding itself so miserably thwarted by the earthly part. Perhaps every man of genius in whatever sphere might recognize the image of his own experience in Aylmer's journal." If this is so, this is the human condition itself, not likely to be cured by adjurations to accept it.

Reflecting further, Georgiana reconsiders the character of Aylmer

and did it completer justice than at any previous moment. Her heart exulted, while it trembled, at his honorable love— so pure and lofty that it would accept nothing less than perfection nor miserably make itself contented with an earthlier nature than he had dreamed of. She felt how much more precious was such a sentiment than that meaner kind which would have borne with the imperfection for her sake, and have been guilty of treason to holy love by degrading its perfect idea to the level of the actual; and with her whole spirit she prayed that, for a single moment, she might satisfy his highest and deepest conception. Longer than one moment she well knew it could not be; for his spirit was ever on the march, ever ascending, and each instant required something that was beyond the scope of the instant before.

This is an expression of purest Romantic dynamism,

*"The Birthmark"*

Whitman's "O farther, farther, farther sail!" or more appropriately still Emerson's

> *Have I a lover noble and free?*
> *I would he were nobler than to love me.*

Unquestionably the passage contains a profound irony, in such phrases as "his honorable love—so pure and lofty," "nor miserably make itself contented with an earthlier nature," "that meaner kind which would have borne with the imperfection for her sake," "been guilty of treason to holy love by degrading its perfect idea," and "with her whole spirit she prayed." But the irony is indeed so deep that it is almost unfathomable; it questions without implying an answer. Aylmer is entangled in great complications, and his problem is treated with great and imaginative sympathy. Hawthorne himself is taken up with the desire of the moth for the star, in despite of the fall.

## X

## *The Scarlet Letter*

INTERPRETATIONS of *The Scarlet Letter* have been almost startlingly various. This is not surprising, for Hawthorne has himself pointed the way to a wide range of speculations. The concluding words of *The Scarlet Letter*, however, summarily dismiss the more cheerful readings, of which there are a number. In describing the heraldic device on the common tombstone of Hester and Dimmesdale, they describe "our now concluded legend; so sombre is it, and relieved only by one ever-glowing point of light gloomier than the shadow:—
'ON A FIELD, SABLE, THE LETTER A, GULES.' "
These words alone, in my opinion, are sufficient evidence for disproving the notion that *The Scarlet Letter* is "about" Hester Prynne the advanced feminist, or that the story can be satisfactorily summarized either by the moral which Hawthorne attaches to Dimmesdale, " 'Show freely to the world, if not your worst, yet some trait whereby the worst may be inferred!' " or by the doctrine of *felix culpa*, "the fortunate fall," that out of sin and evil comes good and that Hester is educated and refined by her wrongdoing. The sentiment is too darkly tragic to be appropriate to any of these conclusions, though Hawthorne at one place and another in *The Scarlet Letter* has suggested the possibility of all of them. The true conclusion of *The Scarlet Letter* is an unre-

solved contradiction—unresolved not from indecision or
lack of thought but from honesty of imagination. Hawthorne gives the only answer that his formulation of the
terms permits. If we consider that the problem of *The
Scarlet Letter* is primarily the problem of Hester Prynne,
the verdict is at best suspension of judgment after full
examination of the evidence. And, as we know, Hester
emerges from trial in better condition than her codefend-
ants Dimmesdale and Chillingworth.

This is the contradiction, and a very widely representative contradiction it is: the sin of *The Scarlet Letter*
is a symbol of the original sin, by which no man is untouched. All mortals commit the sin in one form or another, which is perhaps the meaning of "your worst" in
the exhortation occasioned by the death of Dimmesdale.
Hester, having sinned, makes the best possible recovery;
and the crime itself is of all crimes the most excusable,
coming of passionate love and having "a consecration of
its own." Yet the sin remains real and inescapable, and
she spends her life in retribution, the death of her lover
Dimmesdale having finally taught her that this is the
only way. This is the dilemma: human beings by their
natures must fall into error—and yet it would be better
if they did not.

The letter, an "ever-glowing point of light," is
gloomier than the shadow of its background. The shadow,
the "Field, Sable," is roughly the atmosphere of Puritanism, the "Letter A, Gules" the atmosphere of the sin.
These are at odds, and no absolute superiority is granted
to either. The Puritan doctors are no fit judges of a
woman's heart; nor, on the other hand, is Hester to be
absolved. The letter is glowing, positive, vital, the product of genuine passion, while the sable may certainly be

taken as the negation of everything alive. Yet the letter is gloomier.

These shades are both of hell, and there is no hue of heaven in *The Scarlet Letter* which really offsets them. Sunlight is the nearest approach to it, and its sway is too fleeting to have any great effect. In the forest scene of chapters XVI–XIX sunshine, "as with a sudden smile of heaven," bursts over Hester and Dimmesdale, but this is merely a momentary relief. (The hope which accompanies it is short-lived, delusory, and dangerous) A more steadfast light, "The sun, but little past its meridian," shines down upon Dimmesdale as he stands on the scaffold to confess his guilt. This is triumph, indeed, but little to counterbalance the continual power of the "bale fire" and "lurid gleam" of the letter. Hope and regeneration are sometimes symbolized in Hawthorne by the celestial colors of dawn, transfigured by light: blues, greens, and golds. In "Ethan Brand" the tender hues of the twilight sky are overpowered by night and the red and black of Brand's Unpardonable Sin, but they are revivified by the atmosphere of dawn. So the storm in *The House of the Seven Gables,* which accompanies the crisis and blows itself out with the death of Judge Pyncheon, gives way to a world made new and bathed in morning sunshine. There is no such scene in *The Scarlet Letter.*

The problem of *The Scarlet Letter* can be solved only by introducing the supernatural level of heaven, the sphere of absolute knowledge and justice and—hesitantly—of complete fulfillment. This may seem to be another paradox, and perhaps a disappointing one. Without doubt *The Scarlet Letter* pushes *towards* the limit of moral judgment, suggesting many possible conclusions. It is even relentless in its search in the depths of its characters. There is yet, however, a point beyond which Hawthorne will not go; ultimate solutions are not appropriate in the merely human world. His sympathy with Hester and Dimmesdale is clear enough, but he allows them only to escape the irrevocable spiritual ruin which befalls Chillingworth. Figuratively his good wishes pursue them beyond life, but he does not presume himself to absolve them. Even in the carefully staged scene of Dimdesdale's death, where every impulse of both author and reader demands complete forgiveness, Hawthorne refuses to grant it. With his "bright dying eyes" Dimmesdale looks into eternity, but nothing he sees there permits him to comfort Hester. To her questions, " 'Shall we not meet again? . . . Shall we not spend our immortal life together?' " he can answer only, " 'The law we broke!—the sin here so awfully revealed!—let these alone be in thy thoughts! I fear! I fear!' " A grim and unflinching conclusion, considering everything. Dimmesdale is not of course Hawthorne, but the very preservation of dramatic propriety at this crucial point is significant.

There are four states of being in Hawthorne: one subhuman, two human, and one superhuman. The first is Nature, which comes to our attention in *The Scarlet Letter* twice. It appears first in the opening chapter, in the wild rosebush which stands outside the blackbrowed Puritan jail, and whose blossoms

might be imagined to offer their fragrance and fragile beauty to the prisoner as he went in, and to the condemned criminal as he came forth to his doom, in token that the deep heart of Nature could pity and be kind to him.

The second entrance of Nature comes in the <u>forest scene</u>, <u>where it sympathizes with the forlorn lovers and gives them hope</u>. "Such was the sympathy of Nature—that wild, heathen <u>Nature of the forest, never subjugated by human law, nor illumined by higher truth</u>. . . ." The sentence epitomizes both the virtues of Nature and its inadequacy. <u>In itself good, Nature is not a sufficient support for human beings</u>.

The human levels are represented by Hawthorne's distinction between Heart and Head. The heart is closer to nature, the head to the supernatural. The heart may err by lapsing into nature, which means, since it has not the innocence of nature, into corruption. The danger of the head lies in the opposite direction. It aspires to be superhuman, and is likely to dehumanize itself in the attempt by violating the human limit. Dimmesdale, despite his considerable intellect, is predominantly a heart character, and it is through the heart that sin has assailed him, in a burst of passion which overpowered both religion and reason. The demoniac Chillingworth is of the head, a cold experimenter and thinker. It is fully representative of Hawthorne's general emphasis that Chillingworth's spiritual ruin is complete. Hester Prynne is a combination of head and heart, with a preponderance of head. <u>Her original sin is of passion, but its consequences expose her to the danger of absolute mental isolation</u>. The centrifugal urge of the intellect is counteracted in her by her duty to her daughter Pearl, the product of the sin, and by her latent love for Dimmesdale. <u>Pearl herself is a creature of nature</u>, most at home in the wild forest: ". . . the <u>mother-forest, and these wild things which it nourished, all recognized a kindred wildness in the human child</u>." She is made human by Dimmesdale's confession and death: "The great scene of grief, in which the wild infant bore a part, had developed all her sympathies. . . ."

The fourth level, the superhuman or heavenly, will perhaps merely be confused by elaborate definition. It is the sphere of absolute insight, justice, and mercy. Few of Hawthorne's tales and romances can be adequately considered without taking it into account. As Mark Van Doren has recently emphasized, it is well to remember Hawthorne's belief in immortality. It is because of the very presence of the superhuman in Hawthorne's thinking that the destinies of his chief characters are finally veiled in ambiguity. He respects them as he would have respected any real person by refusing to pass the last judgment, by leaving a residue of mysterious individuality untouched. The whole truth is not for a fellow human to declare.

These four states are not mutually exclusive. Without the touch of nature human life would be too bleak. The Puritans of *The Scarlet Letter* are deficient in nature, and they are consequently dour and overrighteous. Something of the part that nature might play in the best human life is suggested in the early chapters of *The Marble Faun,* particularly through the character Donatello. The defects of either Heart or Head in a state of isolation have already been mentioned. And without some infusion of superhuman meaning into the spheres of the human, life would be worse than bestial. Perhaps only one important character in all of Hawthorne's works finds it possible to dispense completely with heaven—Westervelt, of *The Blithedale Romance*—and he is essentially diabolic. In some respects the highest and the lowest of these levels are most closely akin, as if their relationship were as points of a circle. The innocence of nature is like the innocence of heaven. It is at times, when compared to the human, like the Garden before the serpent, like heaven free of the taint of evil. Like infancy, however, nature is a stage which man must pass through, whereas his destination is heaven. The juxtaposition of highest and lowest nevertheless involves difficulties, when perfect goodness seems equivalent to mere deprivation and virtue seems less a matter of choosing than of being untempted.

The intensity of *The Scarlet Letter*, at which Hawthorne himself was dismayed, comes from concentration, selection, and dramatic irony. The concentration upon the central theme is unremitting. The tension is lessened only once, in the scene in the forest, and then only delusively, since the hope of freedom which brings it about is quickly shown to be false and even sinful. The characters play out their tragic action against a background in itself oppressive—the somber atmosphere of Puritanism. Hawthorne calls the progression of the story "the darkening close of a tale of human frailty and sorrow." Dark to begin with, it grows steadily deeper in gloom. The method is almost unprecedentedly selective. Almost every image has a symbolic function; no scene is superfluous. One would perhaps at times welcome a loosening of the structure, a moment of wandering from the path. The weedy grassplot in front of the prison; the distorting reflection of Hester in a breastplate, where the Scarlet Letter appears gigantic; the tapestry of David and Bathsheba on the wall of the minister's chamber; the little brook in the forest; the slight malformation of Chillingworth's shoulder; the ceremonial procession on election day—in every instance more is meant than meets the eye.

The intensity of *The Scarlet Letter* comes in part from a sustained and rigorous dramatic irony, or irony of situation. This irony arises naturally from the theme of "secret sin," or concealment. "Show freely of your worst," says Hawthorne; the action of *The Scarlet Letter* arises from the failure of Dimmesdale and Chillingworth to do so. The minister hides his sin, and Chillingworth hides his identity. This concealment affords a constant drama. There is the irony of Chapter III, "The Recognition," in which Chillingworth's ignorance is suddenly and blindingly reversed. Separated from his wife by many vicissitudes, he comes upon her as she is dramatically exposed to public infamy. From his instantaneous decision, symbolized by the lifting of his finger to his lips to hide his tie to her, he precipitates the further irony of his sustained hypocrisy.

In the same chapter Hester is confronted with her fellow-adulterer, who is publicly called upon to persuade her as her spiritual guide to reveal his identity. Under the circumstances the situation is highly charged, and his words have a double meaning—one to the onlookers, another far different to Hester and the speaker himself. " 'If thou feelest it to be for thy soul's peace, and that thy earthly punishment will therefore be made more effectual to salvation, I charge thee to speak out the name of thy fellow-sinner and fellow-sufferer!' "

From this scene onward Chillingworth, by living a lie, arouses a constant irony, which is also an ambiguity. With a slight shift in emphasis all his actions can be given a very different interpretation. Seen purely from without, it would be possible to regard him as completely blameless. Hester expresses this ambiguity in Chapter IV, after he has ministered to her sick baby, the product of her faithlessness, with tenderness and skill. " 'Thy acts are like mercy,' " said Hester, bewildered and appalled. 'But thy words interpret thee as a terror!' " Masquerading as a physician, he becomes to Dimmesdale a kind of attendant fiend, racking the minister's soul with constant anguish. Yet outwardly he has done him nothing but good. " 'What evil have I done the man?' asked Roger Chillingworth again. 'I tell thee, Hester Prynne, the richest fee that ever physician earned from monarch could not have bought such care as I have wasted on this miserable priest!' " Even when he closes the way to escape by proposing to take passage on the same ship with the fleeing lovers, it is possible to consider the action merely friendly. His endeavor at the end to hold Dimmesdale back from the saving scaffold is from one point of view reasonable and friendlike, although he is a devil struggling to snatch back an escaping soul. " 'All shall be well! Do not blacken your fame, and perish in dishonor! I can yet save you! Would you bring infamy on your sacred profession?' " Only when Dimmesdale has successfully resisted does Chillingworth openly reveal his purposes. With the physician the culminating irony is that in seeking to damn Dimmesdale he has himself fallen into damnation. As he says in a moment of terrible self-knowledge, " 'A mortal man, with once a human heart, has become a fiend for his especial torment!' " The effect is of an Aristotelian reversal, where a conscious and deep-laid purpose brings about totally unforeseen and opposite results. Chillingworth's relations with Dimmesdale have the persistent fascination of an almost absolute knowledge and power working their will with a helpless victim, a fascination which is heightened by the minister's awareness of an evil close beside him which he cannot place. "All this was accomplished with a subtlety so perfect that the minister, though he had constantly a dim perception of some evil influence watching over him, could never gain a knowledge of its actual nature." It is a classic situation wrought out to its fullest potentialities, in which the reader cannot help sharing the perverse pleasure of the villain.

From the victim's point of view the irony is still deeper, perhaps because we can participate still more fully in his response to it. Dimmesdale, a "remorseful hypocrite," is forced to live a perpetual lie in public. His own considerable talents for self-torture are supplemented by the situation as well as by the devoted efforts of Chillingworth. His knowledge is an agony. His conviction of sin is in exact relationship to the reverence in which his parishioners hold him. He grows pale and meager—it is the asceticism of a saint on earth; his effectiveness as a minister grows with his despair; he confesses the truth in his sermons, but transforms it "into the veriest falsehood" by the generality of his avowal and merely increases the adoration of his flock; every effort deepens his plight, since he will not—until the end—make the effort of complete self-revelation. His great election-day sermon prevails through anguish of heart; to his listeners divinely inspired, its power comes from its undertone of suffering, "the complaint of a human heart, sorrowladen, perchance guilty, telling its secret, whether of guilt or sorrow, to the great heart of mankind. . . ." While Chillingworth at last reveals himself fully, Dimmesdale's secret is too great to be wholly laid bare. His utmost efforts are still partially misunderstood, and "highly respectable witnesses" interpret his death as a culminating act of holiness and humility.

Along with this steady irony of situation there is the

omnipresent irony of the hidden meaning. The author and the reader know what the characters do not. Hawthorne consistently pretends that the coincidence of the action or the image with its significance is merely fortuitous, not planned, lest the effect be spoiled by overinsistence. In other words, he attempts to combine the sufficiently probable with the maximum of arrangement. Thus the waxing and waning of sunlight in the forest scene symbolize the emotions of Hester and Dimmesdale, but we accept this coincidence most easily if we can receive it as chance. Hawthorne's own almost amused awareness of his problem helps us to do so. Yet despite the element of play and the deliberate self-deception demanded, the total effect is one of intensity. Hawthorne is performing a difficult feat with sustained virtuosity in reconciling a constant stress between naturally divergent qualities.

The character of Pearl illuminates this point. Pearl is pure symbol, the living emblem of the sin, a human embodiment of the Scarlet Letter. Her mission is to keep Hester's adultery always before her eyes, to prevent her from attempting to escape its moral consequences. Pearl's childish questions are fiendishly apt; in speech and in action she never strays from the control of her symbolic function; her dress and her looks are related to the letter. When Hester casts the letter away in the forest, Pearl forces her to reassume it by flying into an uncontrollable rage. Yet despite the undeviating arrangement of every circumstance which surrounds her, no single action of hers is ever incredible or inconsistent with the conceivable actions of any child under the same conditions. Given the central improbability of her undeviating purposiveness, she is as lifelike as the brilliantly drawn children of Richard Hughes's *The Innocent Voyage.*

These qualities of concentration, selectivity, and irony, which are responsible for the intensity of *The Scarlet Letter*, tend at their extreme toward excessive regularity and a sense of over-manipulation, although irony is also a counteragent against them. This tendency toward regularity is balanced by Hawthorne's use of ambiguity. The distancing of the story in the past has the effect of ambiguity. Hawthorne so employs the element of time as to warn us that he cannot guarantee the literal truth of his narrative and at the same time to suggest that the essential truth is the clearer; as facts shade off into the background, meaning is left in the foreground unshadowed and disencumbered. The years, he pretends, have winnowed his material, leaving only what is enduring. Tradition and superstition, while he disclaims belief in them, have a way of pointing to truth.

Thus the imagery of hell-fire which occurs throughout *The Scarlet Letter* is dramatically proper to the Puritan background and is attributed to the influence of superstitious legend. It works as relief from more serious concerns and still functions as a symbol of psychological and religious truth. In Chapter III, as Hester is returned from the scaffold to the prison, "It was whispered, by those who peered after her, that the scarlet letter threw a lurid gleam along the dark passage-way of the interior." The imagery of the letter may be summarized by quoting a later passage:

The vulgar, who, in those dreary old times, were always contributing a grotesque horror to what interested their imaginations, had a story about the scarlet letter which we might readily work up into a terrific legend. They averred, that the symbol was not mere scarlet cloth, tinged in an earthly dye-pot, but was red-hot with infernal fire, and could be seen glowing all alight, whenever Hester Pyrnne walked abroad in the nighttime. And we must needs say, it seared Hester's bosom so deeply, that perhaps there was more truth in the rumor than our modern incredulity may be inclined to admit.

The lightness of Hawthorne's tone lends relief and variety, while it nevertheless reveals the function of the superstition. "The vulgar," "dreary old times," "grotesque horror," "work up into a terrific legend"—his scorn is so heavily accented that it discounts itself and satirizes the "modern incredulity" of his affected attitude. The playful extravagance of "red-hot with infernal fire" has the same effect. And the apparent begrudging of the concession in the final sentence—"And we must needs say"—lends weight to a truth so reluctantly admitted.

Puritan demonology is in general used with the same effect. It has the pathos and simplicity of an old wives' tale and yet contains a deep subterranean power which reaches into daylight from the dark caverns of the mind. The Black Man of the unhallowed forest—a useful counterbalance to any too-optimistic picture of nature—and the witchwoman Mistress Hibbins are cases in point. The latter is a concrete example of the mingled elements of the superstitious legend. Matter-of-factly, she is a Puritan lady of high rank, whose ominous reputation is accounted for by bad temper combined with insanity. As a witch, she is a figure from a child's storybook, an object of delighted fear and mockery. Yet her fanciful extravagance covers a real malignity, and because of it she has an insight into the secret of the letter. With one stroke she lays bare the disease in Dimmesdale, as one who sees evil alone but sees it with unmatched acuteness: " 'When the Black Man sees one of his own servants, signed and sealed, so shy of owning to the bond as is the Reverend Mr. Dimmesdale, he hath a way of ordering matters so that the mark shall be disclosed to the eyes of all the world.' "

This use of the past merges into a deep-seated ambiguity of moral meaning. Moral complexity and freedom of speculation, like the lighter ambiguity of literal fact, temper the almost excessive unity and symmetry of *The Scarlet Letter* and avoid a directed verdict. In my opinion the judgment of Hawthorne upon his characters is entirely clear, although deliberately limited in its jurisdiction. But he permits the possibility of other interpretations to appear, so that the consistent clarity of his own emphasis is disguised. Let us take for example the consideration of the heroine in Chapter XIII, "Another View of Hester." After seven years of disgrace, Hester has won the unwilling respect of her fellow-townsmen by her good works and respectability of conduct. From one point of view she is clearly their moral superior: she has met rigorous cruelty with kindness, arrogance with humility. Furthermore, living as she has in enforced isolation has greatly developed her mind. In her breadth of intellectual speculation she has freed herself from any dependence upon the laws of Puritan society. "She cast away the fragments of a broken chain." She pays outward obedience to a system which has no further power upon her spirit. Under other conditions, Hawthorne suggests, she might at this juncture have become another Anne Hutchinson, the foundress of a religious sect, or a great early feminist. The author's conclusions about these possibilities, however, are specifically stated: "The scarlet letter had not done its office." Hester is wounded and led

145

astray, not improved, by her situation. Hawthorne permits his reader, if he wishes, to take his character from his control, to say that Hester Prynne is a great woman unhappily born before her time, or that she is a good woman wronged by her fellow men. But Hawthorne is less confident.

In the multiple interpretations which constitute the moral ambiguities of *The Scarlet Letter* there is no clear distinction of true and false, but there *is* a difference between superficial and profound. In instances where interpretation of observed fact fuses with interpretation of moral meaning, conclusions are generally relative to those who make them. After Dimmesdale's climactic death scene

Most of the spectators testified to having seen, on the breast of the unhappy minister, a SCARLET LETTER—the very semblance of that worn by Hester Prynne—imprinted in the flesh. As regarded its origin, there were various explanations, all of which must necessarily have been conjectural. Some affirmed that the Reverend Mr. Dimmesdale, on the very day when Hester Pyrnne first wore her ignominious badge, had begun a course of penance,—which he afterwards, in so many futile methods, followed out,—by inflicting a hideous torture on himself. Others contended that the stigma had not been produced until a long time subsequent, when old Roger Chillingworth, being a potent necromancer, had caused it to appear, through the agency of magic and poisonous drugs. Others, again,—and those best able to appreciate the minister's peculiar sensibility, and the wonderful operation of his spirit upon the body,—whispered their belief, that the awful symbol was the effect of the ever-active tooth of remorse, gnawing from the inmost heart outwardly, and at last manifesting Heaven's dreadful judgment by the visible presence of the letter.

Most singular is the fact that some spectators have seen no letter at all.

The presence of so many possibilities hints strongly that the whole truth is not to be found in any single choice, but Hawthorne's own preference is clearly indicated by "those best able to appreciate."

In a different case all interpretations are equally false, or at least equally erring. In Chapter XII, "The Minister's Vigil," a meteor flashes across the sky, which to the morbid eye of Dimmesdale takes the form of a gigantic *A*. This vision is attributed to the disordered mental state of the minister, though we cannot accept even this disclaimer with complete simplicity. This being the night of Governor Winthrop's death, one good old Puritan interprets the portent as *A* for Angel—an observation which has the effect of giving objective support to Dimmesdale's vision.

There is also the ambivalence of the Puritans. It is easy to pass them by too quickly. One's first impression is doubtless, as Hawthorne says elsewhere, of a set of "dismal wretches," but they are more than this. The Puritan code is arrogant, inflexible, overrighteous; and it is remarked of their magistrates and priests that "out of the whole human family, it would not have been easy to select the same number of wise and virtuous persons, who should be less capable of sitting in judgment on an erring woman's heart. . . ." Nevertheless, after finishing *The Scarlet Letter* one might well ask what merely human society would be better. With all its rigors, the ordeal of Hester upon the scaffold is invested with awe by the real seriousness and simplicity of the onlookers. Hawthorne compares the Puritan attitude, and certainly not unfavorably, to "the heartlessness of another social state, which would find only a theme for jest in an exhibition like the present." And it is counted as a virtue that the chief men of the town attend the spectacle without loss of dignity. Without question they take upon themselves more of the judgment of the soul than is fitting for men to assume, but this fault is palliated by their complete sincerity. They are "a people amongst whom religion and law were almost identical, and in whose character both were so thoroughly interfused, that the mildest and the severest acts of public discipline were alike made venerable and awful." By any ideal standard they are greatly lacking, but among erring humans they are, after all, creditable.

Furthermore, the vigor of Hawthorne's abuse of them is not to be taken at face value. They are grim, grisly, stern-browed and unkindly visaged; amid the gaiety of election day "for the space of a single holiday, they appeared scarcely more grave than most other communities at a period of general affliction." In this statement the tone of good-humored mockery is unmistakable. Hawthorne's attacks have something of the quality of a family joke; their roughness comes from thorough and even affectionate understanding. As his excellent critic and son-in-law G. P. Lathrop long ago pointed out, Hawthorne is talking of his own people and in hitting at them is quite conscious that he hits himself.

Finally, the pervasive influence of Hawthorne's style modifies the rigorous and purposeful direction of the action and the accompanying symmetrical ironies. The style is urbane, relaxed, and reposeful and is rarely without some touch of amiable and unaccented humor. This quality varies, of course, with the situation. Hester exposed on the scaffold and Dimmesdale wracked by Chillingworth are not fit subjects for humor. Yet Hawthorne always preserves a measure of distance, even at his most sympathetic. The effect of Hawthorne's prose comes partly from generality, in itself a factor in maintaining distance, as if the author at his most searching chose always to preserve a certain reticence, to keep to what is broadly representative and conceal the personal and particular. Even the most anguished emotion is clothed with decency and measure, and the most painful situations are softened by decorum.

## XI

# *The House of the Seven Gables*

As with *The Scarlet Letter, The House of the Seven Gables* is concerned with the effects of an evil action, this time prolonged over generations. As in *The Scarlet Letter*, the act cannot be recalled—in this world there is no annulment, no wiping the slate clean until the original sin has worked itself out. The sin of Colonel Pyncheon was greed, coupled with a false and wrongful desire to live through his posterity. Seeking to enrich his line, he brought a curse on them instead. "Maule's Curse" loses its potency only after Clifford and Hepzibah Pyncheon, innocent persons separated by many generations from the Puritan Colonel, have bitterly suffered for the greater part of their lives.

This study in the continuity of guilt links the primary theme very closely with the secondary theme: conservatism and the new spirit of radical democracy. The Pyncheons are fighting to maintain a state of isolated superiority over their fellows in society, an endeavor against which the society of *The House of the Seven Gables* has set its face. The original sin was committed with this end in view, and it is perpetuated by the Pyncheon line for the same reason, until there is no longer a Pyncheon who will renew the struggle. This battle of old and new is not wholly one-sided. Its final issue, in fact, is so modulated as to be very difficult to describe exactly. While it is clear that false family pride and gentility are condemned, since they arise from a materialistic conception of family honor and prosperity, it would also appear that it is only through family ties—of nature, of instinct, and of heart—that there is meaning and continuity in life. If the bases beneath the Pyncheons had been good, the results might also have been good. It is possible too, however, that a merely human continuity is preserved only through such means as the Pyncheons used, that every human organism contains within itself germs of corruption and death.

Consider the conclusion of *The House of the Seven Gables*. The Pyncheons have died in the person of Judge Pyncheon, the re-embodiment of the original sinner and founder of the family and the representative of its determining force. God, in accordance with the curse, has given him blood to drink. Clifford and Hepzibah Pyncheon survive but live out their days in a calm Indian summer of happiness, without further influence or action. They are both childless. The family survives and continues in Phoebe Pyncheon, who is not in the direct line. Phoebe has been removed from the atmosphere of the Pyncheons by the defection of her father, "who married a young woman of no family or property, and died in very poor circumstances." A thread of continuity will presumably be maintained by her marriage to Holgrave, the "new man" and radical democrat. It would seem, then, that the Pyncheons are to go on, though purged of pride and even the family name—purged, indeed, of everything that went with the idea of Pyncheon. They do not wholly disappear. There is irony in the fact that Holgrave is really a Maule, a member of the wronged family who pronounced the curse and were the Pyncheons' ancient enemies. It will be noticed that one irony is complicated and foregone by Holgrave's change of name; "Pyncheon" might have become "Maule" but instead starts afresh with a name unentangled by the web of the past.

But it is surely significant that the new man Holgrave is new wine in an old bottle, the member of a family as old as the Pyncheons themselves, thus representing an equal though different continuity. And Holgrave's root-and-branch radicalism, which would commence every generation afresh and purify with fire the house of the seven gables "till only its ashes remain," is thoroughly modified by his first really human tie, his love for Phoebe. At the end we find him actually reproaching the late Judge Pyncheon—"being so opulent, and with a reasonable prospect of transmitting his wealth to descendants of his own"—for failing to build his country house in stone, rather than in wood. What a sentiment!

The family of the Maules, which stubbornly survives in Holgrave, is an obvious contrast with the Pyncheons. The Pyncheons are aristocrats, the Maules as persistently plebeian: carpenters, artisans, sailors before the mast. Their continuity is subterranean; Matthew Maule's posterity "was supposed now to be extinct." "For thirty years past, neither town-record, nor gravestone, nor the directory, nor the knowledge or memory of man, bore any trace of Matthew Maule's descendants." From these underground rivers they arise once more in the fresh and vigorous Holgrave. They are likely to end their days in almshouses, casting themselves perforce upon the mercy of society, after obscure lives spent "in hired tenements." Compared to the Pyncheons they are thus both rooted and rootless, closer to the great mass of humanity, yet never presuming to lay a claim to any such symbol of possession as the house of the seven gables. It must be said that they are not fully representative of "the common man"; they do not wholly yield themselves to the bosom of society. They have their own isolation, the reproach of the taint of the wizard, "an hereditary character of reserve" which perhaps by making them difficult to aid has added to their misfortunes. This reserve is a product of the original crime against them and is imposed upon them rather than innate. Thus it is another evil to be entered against the Pyncheons. If so, it is another instance of the complexity of Hawthorne's moral situations, in which the guiltless victims as well as the criminals suffer spiritual harm.

The Pyncheons sin by spiritual pride, of which their greed is both the symptom and the instrument. The penalty of their sin is a materialistic delusion centering itself in their claim upon the Eastern Lands of Waldo County, Maine, which for generations fills them with ducal or princely aspirations. "This impalpable claim . . . resulted in nothing more solid than to cherish, from generation to generation, an absurd delusion of family importance, which all along characterized the Pyncheons." The meaning of this claim is pointed by the final discovery of the documents, now fairy gold, completely worthless. This meaning is reinforced by the further circumstance that Judge Pyncheon, the practical man of business, has been led to confuse these worthless relics with the remains of his uncle's fortune, which have inexplicably disappeared and are actually nonexistent. Throughout the novel his whole action, the result of an ambiguous remark of Clifford's, is based upon his pursuit of the elusive money. Thus he repeats the original error of the Pyncheons, as he has repeated the original sin.

Through pride the Pyncheons have sought to isolate themselves; through pride and delusion they fall. The Maules have paid their way as they went and have their eventual triumph, qualified though it be. Humble folk, though courageous, they have not tempted the thunderer's hand. They have survived, perhaps, from a matter-of-factness which has the effect of forbearance. The builder of the house of the seven gables was actually the son of Matthew Maule, working for hire for his father's undoer, though by the same token it was he who hid the documents of the Eastern Lands. The fable runs that the Maules, ill as they fare in the actual, hold the Pyncheons as thralls in the world of dreams, "the topsy-turvy commonwealth of sleep" (and this story is suggestive as a criticism of values); but in daylight they do not presume to enmity. It is one of the strengths of Holgrave that he is less touched by ancient wrong than are the Pyncheons.

The principal characters of *The House of the Seven Gables* are Hepzibah, Clifford, Phoebe, and Judge Jaffrey Pyncheon; and Holgrave. Hepzibah, the real heroine of the book, is an unattractive, almost grotesque old maid. She is both symbol and victim of the old order, sheltered and weakened as well by its unbased gentility. She is a soul led astray, wandering in a maze, estranged from life by inherited and vicarious guilt which in its contemporary manifestation has wreaked itself upon her brother Clifford through her cousin Jaffrey. She and Clifford win to safety only through the aid of Phoebe and Holgrave, who are uninfluenced by the house and the curse. She stands amid her weakness for the strength of love, by which she is preserved and ennobled. She is a reminder of the complexity of moral meaning and of life itself in the discrepancy between her appearance, which is darkened by a perpetual nearsighted scowl, and her real nature, which is not only loving but lofty. She is extremely interesting, as a tragic character with the untragic flaw of physical absurdity. She strikes the note Hawthorne intentionally seeks—a note of intensity which can at intervals be slackened and diffused, since he seeks to avoid the unrelieved "hell fire" tone of *The Scarlet Letter* by an apparent (though deceptive) interest in casual detail.

Clifford, her unfortunate brother, who represents pure aesthetic sensibility, has been mutilated by contact with the Pyncheon curse. Exquisitely fitted to appreciate all that is pleasant in life, he has spent many years in a prison cell on a false conviction engineered by his cousin Jaffrey. Because of his lack of other necessary human qualities, his great gift of sensibility is dangerous to himself.

Of all the characters of *The House of the Seven Gables* Phoebe Pyncheon is closest to the center of human nature. A conservative in the best sense, she represents the truth of the heart. She is the best of human ties and human feelings. She has far less moral depth than Hepzibah, to whom she is as a child to a woman; she is less sensitive than Clifford, and much less intelligent than Holgrave; but Hawthorne represents her as of greater power than any of these, through an instinctive but consummate talent for everyday living. She presents a contradiction recurrent in Hawthorne: in portraying her he must condescend to some extent, although reluctantly. She has qualities which he regards as humanly perfect, but on another level he is unsatisfied and is forced to an uneasy self-restraint.

Holgrave is the "new man," the democrat at his best, yet possessed of flaws as well as virtues. In his haste he would destroy much that is good along with the evil; and Hawthorne has elsewhere expressed his belief, as in "Earth's Holocaust," that evil is coincident with the human heart and will last while it lasts. Radicalism therefore is always fallacious; it has not found the secret of sweeping the Augean stables. Holgrave as he is first presented to us is a man of the head or intellect, with the intellect's shortcomings. His well-meant universal philanthropy would eradicate all human warmth, idiosyncrasies, relationships—all that is represented by the heart, in fact. Characteristically he is a Yankee jack-of-all-trades. At twenty-two he has been a salesman, a schoolmaster, an editor, a peddler, a dentist, a supercargo, a Fourierist, and a lecturer on mesmerism; at the moment he is a daguerreotypist. This diversity suggests his deliberate rootlessness, which is as absolute as his own will can make it. His present occupation is of some significance. F. O. Matthiessen has remarked upon the value of Holgrave's pictures, which are produced in the medium of clear daylight, as penetrations of truth. His picture of Judge Pyncheon unerringly reveals, for instance, all that the Judge conceals. Yet this medium can hardly be adequate, particularly for a writer so interested in depth and chiaroscuro as Hawthorne. His daguerreotypes, like Holgrave's own vision, for which they are a symbol, are clear but limited. One doubts that Holgrave could produce a just likeness of Hepzibah.

Holgrave and Jaffrey Pyncheon are the two strong men of the story, but Holgrave's urge to power is controlled by a fundamental morality. The Judge's talent and his lust are directed to the material, for which he has a grasp and an urge unqualified by humanity. The spiritual peril of Holgrave resides in his intellect. He is daringly speculative, prone to wander far from the safe center of things. He has more than a hint of the cold, analytical curiosity of Ethan Brand, which if it conquers leads to the Unpardonable Sin. His status as a roomer in the house of the seven gables indicates his position. He is dangerously near to viewing the emotions and sorrows of Clifford and Hepzibah as a mere intellectual treat, from the point of view of an amused and unloving spectator. If this were wholly true, it would in Hawthorne be damning. Of the house he says, "I am pursuing my studies here."

His dangerous curiosity and his potential power are both contained within his gift of mesmerism, which is for Hawthorne a violation of the human spirit. Holgrave's control and consequent salvation, however, are pointed out in Chapter XIV, in which he resists the temptation to influence Phoebe when she accidentally comes under his power. His refusal is made more dramatic by the fact that he has just been telling the story of Matthew Maule, who in a parallel situation took full advantage of his power over Alice Pyncheon.

To a disposition like Holgrave's, at once speculative and active, there is no temptation so great as the opportunity of acquiring empire over the human spirit; nor any idea more seductive to a young man than to become the arbiter of a young girl's destiny. Let us, therefore,—whatever his defects of nature and education, and in spite of his scorn for creeds and institutions,—concede to the daguerreotypist the rare and high quality of reverence for another's individuality. Let us allow him integrity, also, forever after to be confided in; since he forbade himself to twine that one link more which might have rendered his spell over Phoebe indissoluble.

The ultimate union of Holgrave and Phoebe is symbolically the ideal union of head and heart, centripetal and centrifugal forces in perfect balance. Typically with Hawthorne, however, the union is a balance rather than a synthesis. Holgrave, rather than being made perfect, loses to gain. One need not feel that he loses wholly his adventurous daring, but the emphasis is on the curbing of it.

Judge Pyncheon, the one evil person in *The House of the Seven Gables,* is the embodiment of Pyncheon pride and greed, the original Puritan reincarnated in the nineteenth century. He is dehumanized by his preoccupation with "the big, heavy, solid unrealities, such as gold, landed estate, offices of trust and emolument, and public honors," which he possesses "vast ability in grasping." Hawthorne compares his life to "a sculptured and ornamented pile of ostentatious deeds," beneath which is buried "some evil and unsightly thing"; and again to a stately palace, in which somewhere lies a corpse, "half-decayed, and still decaying, and diffusing its death-scent." These images imply what is elsewhere specifically stated; the Judge is little conscious of his own evil. Some five minutes of the day, it may be, of "some black day in the whole year's circle," he knows himself. For the rest, his conscience is enviably clear. He is, in fact, a study in the discrepancy of appearance and reality, a hypocrite himself deceived, who is taken generally at face value. His outward actions wear consistently the face of virtue, as judge, politician, agriculturist, and householder. Even his crimes are ambiguous. He betrays Clifford by a simple omission, and his carefully plotted intention of consigning his cousin to a madhouse could be taken for mercy: " 'From all this testimony, I am led to apprehend—reluctantly, and with deep grief—that Clifford's misfortunes have so affected his intellect, never very strong, that he cannot safely remain at large.' " Impregnably respectable, he is truly known only by Hepzibah and by the secret murmur of the human heart, which expresses itself in gossip and scandal. As tradition has preserved dark stories of his ancestor the Colonel while conventional history speaks him fair, so does the "private diurnal gossip" about the Judge have him greedy, proud, lustful, and remorselessly cruel.

Judge Pyncheon is dehumanized by his exclusive preoccupation with the material. The principles of disproportion and excess are fundamental in him and are the source of his evil. His materialism is figured in his huge physical bulk. A study of Hawthorne's imagery will show that he is not unfavorable to physical massiveness, whether of architecture or of flesh; indeed, Dr. Johnson is a favorite of his. But disproportioned mass is horrible to him, as may be seen in his notorious attack on well-fed English womanhood in *The English Notebooks*. This excess appears also in the recurrent images of sun and storm which accompany Judge Pyncheon. His false and outer self is clothed in a sunlike benevolence, "and, like the sun, he shines on all alike." This sun, his normal guise, is too hot for comfort, however. Phoebe finds herself "quite overpowered by the sultry, dog-day heat, as it were, of benevolence, which this excellent man diffused out of his great heart into the surrounding atmosphere." Pursuing the conceit, Hawthorne attributes to him "a smile, so broad and sultry, that, had it been only half as warm as it looked, a trellis of grapes might at once have turned purple under its summer-like exposure. It may have been his purpose, indeed, to melt poor Hepzibah on the spot, as if she were a figure of yellow wax." His true nature, on the other hand, is imaged in a thundercloud, sudden in appearance and especially shocking by contrast. "It was quite as striking, allowing for the difference of scale, as that [change] betwixt a landscape under a broad sunshine and just before a thunder-storm; not that it had the passionate intensity of the latter aspect, but was cold, hard, immitigable, like a day-long brooding cloud."

As a portrait Judge Pyncheon is not wholly successful. In conveying excess and disproportion Hawthorne is sometimes himself led into them. He pursues his character with an attitude akin to hatred, which manifests itself in a too persistent and obtrusive irony. This irony quite naturally accompanies the antithesis of appearance and reality, but it is carried to the point of monotony. In the famous scene of the Judge's death it rises to intensity and passion; elsewhere the situations are too delicate to sustain it. This relative failure comes from Hawthorne's lack of sympathy with his creation. The complete materialist, who is deluded by appearance and attempts to become appearance himself, is much less attractive to Hawthorne than the opposite, the man of pure intellect led astray by speculation. Westervelt of *The Blithedale Romance,* for example, offers less opportunity to insight than Ethan Brand, or Chillingworth, or even Rappaccini. These extremes meet, we may remark, in a common abstraction and disregard for human values.

Nevertheless, Judge Pyncheon is striking as an evocation of the power of evil, a power which is projected by images of mass, of darkness, and of hardness. He is "iron-hearted." To oppose him with the unfortunate Clifford "would be like flinging a porcelain vase, with already a crack in it, against a granite column." The Judge is "powerful by intellect, energy of will, the long habit of acting among men, and . . . by his unscrupulous pursuit of selfish ends through evil means." The more human Hepzibah and Clifford are powerless against him; he is defeated only by the hereditary enemy of the Pyncheons, death by apoplexy.

The Judge is brought precisely to the apex of his career as a practical man. As a logical outcome of careful planning, he is about to win complete victory over Clifford and Hepzibah, and his public life is to be crowned by the nomination for governor. Then retribution overtakes him. At the recurrence of "Maule's curse," the obvious symmetry of the form of retribution is likely to divert attention from the fitness of the symbol. Pyncheon's death is the outward costume of bitter spiritual conflict. He is a human being after all, and is killed by a force within him. His death, designedly in the chamber and chair of his Puritan prototype, is foreshadowed by the hint of this internal force:

. . . it may be that no wearier and sadder man had ever sunk into the chair than this same Judge Pyncheon, whom we have just beheld so immitigably hard and resolute. Surely, it must have been at no slight cost that he had thus fortified his soul with iron. Such calmness is a mightier effort than the violence of weaker men. And there was yet a heavy task for him to do.

His ending is no superficial nicety of plot but rises from himself.

The house itself is a symbol more comprehensive than any of the human characters. The house of the seven gables is not quite spacious enough to contain the world, but it is adequate to hold the considerable problems of the Pyncheons. As in Poe's "The Fall of the House of Usher," family and house are interchangeable. From the first the dwelling is made human: "The aspect of the venerable mansion has always affected me like a human countenance, bearing the traces not merely of outward storm and sunshine, but expressive, also, of the long lapse of mortal life, and accompanying vicissitudes that have passed within." Its "aspect," then, shows the effects of time, mortality, and vicissitude, through the outer envelope of physical weathering. It is a living, sentient organism, "like a great human heart, with a life of its own, and full of rich and sombre reminiscences." Its "great chimney in the centre" is made to represent a heart, which warms and unifies the entire structure, making "a great whole" of the smaller units of the seven gables.

There is much that is good and venerable about the Pyncheon past. The long years of mortality have been human and warming as well as dark. The strands of existence which the old house comprises are many and complexly intertangled. Here we might consider the effects of weathering and time. The mansion is more than once described as "weather-beaten." The "green moss that had long since gathered over the projections of the windows" has a softening grace and is valuable in giving the house a place in nature; the giant burdocks which grow in "enormous fertility" in the yard and the angles of the building are unwholesome and ominous. Time has made the house "black in the prevalent east wind"—"the dreaded east"

—but permitted "some spots of more verdant mossiness." It is venerable with the sense of the past, but it is also almost deadly. It is intimately acquainted with dust and decay, "unwholesome for the lungs," and with sordid grime. The genial temperament of Phoebe combats its "grime and sordidness," its dry rot, its "heavy, breathless scent" of death. Clifford, in a moment of defiance, calls it " 'a rusty, crazy, creaky, dry-rotted, damp-rotted, dingy, dark, and miserable old dungeon.' "

The house is dark, secret, and heavy-browed from the projection of the upper stories over the lower, which casts a "shadowy and thoughtful gloom into the lower rooms," a frown a little like the Judge's and perhaps a little like Hepzibah's. Pleasanter is the Pyncheon elm, which even more than the moss is a connecting link with nature, bringing the house to its merciful fellowship. "It gave beauty to the old edifice, and seemed to make it a part of nature." "Alice's Posies," growing high between gables, are a further link with nature, and by their position and their association with the best of the Pyncheon past they have a still broader significance. Crimson-spotted, they are used with a smooth irony to signalize the Judge's death. "They were flaunting in rich beauty and full bloom to-day, and seemed, as it were, a mystic expression that something within the house was consummated."

The darkness of the house is evil. The dead Judge sits amid darkness and storm—brought by the east wind. The clearing of the moral atmosphere is symbolized by the gradual lessening of dark, preluded by the veering of the wind to the northwest. Starlight appears, then moonlight, transforming the dark with a "silvery dance." Morning transfigures the old mansion: "It would have been enough to live for, merely to look up at the wide benediction of the sky . . . genial once more with sunshine. . . . there was really an inviting aspect over the venerable edifice, conveying an idea that its history must be a decorous and happy one. . . ."

The garden, like the house, epitomizes the Pyncheon story and contains both good and evil. It is an Eden, subtly tainted; its black, rich mold has a flavor of the churchyard and the sexton's spade; its beautiful white roses have mildew at the heart. In it is Maule's well, once sweet, but now "water bewitched" and dangerous to drink since the time of the old Colonel. Over it, too, Nature has cast its healing influence in the robins and the bees which have honored it with their presence. The good offices of Phoebe and Holgrave are shown at work here, checking the spread of weeds and cultivating more wholesome growths. On her first visit to the garden, Phoebe notices the results of Holgrave's labor. "The evil of these departed years would naturally have sprung up again, in such rank weeds (symbolic of the transmitted vices of society) as are always prone to root themselves about human dwellings. Phoebe saw, however, that their growth must have been checked by a degree of careful labor, bestowed daily and systematically on the garden." This good effect is paralleled by Phoebe's influence upon Hepzibah and Clifford, themselves afflicted by the same ills from which the garden suffers.

To return to the house: its evil is visually centered in the portrait, the chair, and the chamber of the old Colonel, all of which are infused with darkness. Of the portrait it is said, "Those stern, immitigable features seemed to symbolize an evil influence, and so darkly to mingle the shadow of their presence with the sunshine of the passing hour, that no good thoughts or purposes could ever spring up and blossom here." The room is curtained, low-studded, panelled with dark wood, and sheltered beneath the brow of the projecting second story. The very chairs suggest the ill effects of the Pyncheon past upon the Pyncheon present, being "straight and stiff, and so ingeniously contrived for the discomfort of the human person that they were irksome even to sight, and conveyed the ugliest possible idea of the state of society to which they could have been adapted." This room, the evil principle of the house, is directly opposed to the human, warming, heartlike principle of good which is represented by the huge, clustered chimney.

In consonance with the tone of *The House of the Seven Gables,* but with a certain absurdity allaying its dignity, is the little shop which resides beneath the front gable and strikes a jarring note in the old mansion's impressiveness. The little shop-bell rings out with a spiteful, mocking tone, jeering at Pyncheon pride and pretensions. Hepzibah is forced by poverty to keep a "cent shop," and this too is prepared for her by the Pyncheon past, in which an ancestor so forgot himself as to become a shopkeeper, although forced in tending his shop to turn back the ruffles from his wrist. The story of the Pyncheons, after all, is not the story of a ducal house. There is something out of keeping in their attempts at aristocratic isolation. The house is not a palace; in the interpolated story of Alice Pyncheon her father finds it "exceedingly inadequate to the style of living which it would be incumbent on Mr. Pyncheon to support, after realizing his territorial rights." The shop, then, represents a quality of the house; it portrays a joint in the Pyncheon armor; and it shows, as in an inverted perspective, the true origins of the Pyncheon fortunes and values, divested of their usual trappings.

There is one further remarkable feature of the house: the arched window which overlooks the street from the second story. This window is the eye of the house, and from here Clifford views secretly the pageantry of passing life and looks down at the small eddies of a current from which he is forever isolated. It is from here that, excited by a procession ("a mighty river of life . . . calling to the kindred depth within him"), he is on the verge of plunging suicidally "into the surging stream of human sympathies."

The power of the house is the isolating force of the crime and the past. Clifford's attempt to escape we have just mentioned. On another occasion he and Hepzibah strive to break the spell by starting for church to re-enter human society, but scarcely pass their own door. Trembling and exposed, they flee within in an uncontrollable revulsion. They themselves cannot escape. In their most serious effort, impelled by shock at the death of the Judge, they go so far as to take a train, which in its rootlessness is the antithesis of the house. For the moment Clifford finds a wild sense of release and exhilaration, which has its vent in wild, half-maniacal talk. But even here he refers obsessedly to " 'a dark, low, cross-beamed, panelled room of an old house,' " with " 'a dead man, sitting in an arm-chair, with a blood-stain on his shirt-bosom' "—the epitome of all the evil of the Pyncheon past. Their freedom is only "the freedom of a broken law," momentary and delusory, like Dimmesdale's wild freedom as he returns from the forest in *The Scarlet Letter*. One wonders if it is only coincidence that Clifford's bubble bursts immediately after the train passes a "wooden church, black with age, and in a dismal state of ruin and decay," and an old farmhouse "as venerably black as the church." These are forcible warnings that the past is inescapable.

Finally there are the resemblances between the house and the Judge, the embodiment of Pyncheon evil. First, there is the relation of the Colonel's portrait, of which the Judge is a modern reincarnation. Judge and house are alike in physical massiveness—the house is "ponderously framed"—and in physical darkness. The Judge is notably dark and sallow; when he attempts to kiss the sunshiny Phoebe, she is especially repelled by his swarthiness. Most important of all, the two are linked by the image of the buried corpse beneath a handsome building. The Judge's life, as was earlier noticed, is thus pictured; while the house was built upon the buried Maule, it concealed the secret of the dead Colonel and ironically is to conceal the hidden corpse of the Judge himself. It seems a fine touch that the Judge in his practical wisdom has no interest in the house but dwells in a pleasant modern country estate. Rejecting, as a man of affairs, a mere outworn symbol, he rejects in it all that is good and human without evading the evil.

# XII

## *The Blithedale Romance*

THE TWO THEMES of *The Blithedale Romance* are interrelated. The tragic theme of the human heart is dominant, but it is supported by the secondary interest of the Blithedale Utopian experiment, which was, of course, suggested by Hawthorne's own experience at Brook Farm. The latter does not constitute a fully developed action, but our retrospective knowledge of the downfall of the Blithedale experiment blends with Zenobia's disaster. Hawthorne's account of this experiment is generous and affectionate, yet decisive at last, and its issues arouse his constant preoccupation with the conflicting claims of the past and the future. He concludes that in the nature of the world the death of this project was inevitable, yet the attempt has enlarged the boundaries of the human spirit. The error of the Blithedale reformers, like the error of the radical Holgrave in *The House of the Seven Gables,* lies not in the desire or the effort for improvement, but in an overestimation of its possible boundaries and in an underestimation of the time it would take to achieve it. Man will not, like Shelley's snake in *Hellas,* cast off his winter weeds and suddenly emerge new-clothed. The process consists rather of patching the old garment as it wears away. The Blithedale venture is valuable as a single item of credit in a complex computation of good and evil.

The downfall of Blithedale echoes the main action
through the theme of tragic waste—so much of human
worth and goodness cast prodigally away. The queenly
Zenobia kills herself, the potentialities of Coverdale are
thwarted, the bright hopes of the experiment are blighted. It is notable that these failures are linked by a common lapse of faith and insight. The root of Zenobia's
tragedy lies in her failure to rise beyond materialism,
which, embodied in Westervelt, deceives her; Blithedale
lapses into the dead materiality of Fourierism.

Our interest is at first directed primarily toward the
experiment, which gradually gives way to the more concrete and individual problems of Zenobia, Hollingsworth, and Priscilla. These characters constitute a criticism of Blithedale. In the truth and heat of passion the
milieu of the experiment is dreamlike and unreal, as when
the story's climax occurs in the midst of a holiday masquerade. From the vantage point of the sinful heart
Blithedale looks somehow false, self-consciously pastoral
and Arcadian.

The time scheme of *The Blithedale Romance* also
comments upon setting and action and is an important
element of structure. The book commences in spring, as
is fitting for so hopeful a project. But the April day is
sadly unseasonable; the new life begins coldly in a driv-
ing snowstorm. The storm is all that is hostile: the reformers take refuge by a blazing household fire, which
"so cheered our spirits that we cared not what inclemency
might rage and roar on the other side of our illuminated
windows." This fire, generous and warming as it is, is
the work of amateurs and immediately sets Blithedale
apart from its social milieu. "The exuberance of this
household fire would alone have sufficed to bespeak us

no true farmers; for the New England yeoman, if he have the misfortune to dwell within practicable distance of a wood-market, is as niggardly of each stick as if it were a bar of California gold." The stormy hostility of nature is underlined by its effect upon the city-bred Priscilla, who flinches at each creak and puff of wind. "The house probably seemed to her adrift on the great ocean of the night." "How cold an Arcadia was this!" comments the narrator Coverdale. We need not enlarge upon the fact that, fresh from a comfortable city apartment, he wakes next morning with pneumonia.

In *The Blithedale Romance* the seasons move in a regular and formal march. Coverdale rises on May Day from his sickbed to look about upon his "Modern Arcadia." The power and intensity of summer, like the vivid Zenobia, cast doubt upon the experiment simply by existing. The "sensual influence in the broad light of noon" produces "a mood of disbelief in moral beauty or heroism, and a conviction of the folly of attempting to benefit the world." Beneath the hot summer sun the earth, like a priestess, offers up incense, but in an alien worship. Coverdale leaves Blithedale in August, driven away by the heat of personal involvements and emotions. "The sunburnt and arid aspect of our woods and pastures, beneath the August sky, did but imperfectly symbolize the lack of dew and moisture, that, since yesterday, had blighted my fields of thought. . . ." Catastrophe and denouement occur in September, which is glorified with crimson and gold but is dying, too. The movement is definite, heavy, and ritualistic, like a ceremonial dance which celebrates a myth.

In this effect the theme of Arcadia plays an important part. Blithedale is an Arcadia exposed to the criticism of nature, of economics and society, and of human passion. It sometimes seems merely a stage pastoral, "an unsubstantial sort of business." In Chapter VIII, "A Modern Arcadia," Coverdale emerges from his sickroom to find reality transfigured. "In my new enthusiasm, man looked strong and stately,—and woman, oh how beautiful!—and the earth a green garden, blossoming with many-colored delights." However, the chapter title is partly ironic. The colonists, who envision a "spiritualization of labor" which "was to be our form of prayer and ceremonial of worship," find themselves stultified instead. "Our labor symbolized nothing, and left us mentally sluggish in the dusk of the evening." Thus the ritual is in danger of being an empty form. The tragic action is forced by the Arcadianism of Blithedale, in which human relations are different from the relationships of conventional society and are thus potentially dangerous. "While inclining us to the soft affections of the golden age, it seemed to authorize any individual, of either sex, to fall in love with any other, regardless of what would elsewhere be judged suitable and prudent." The cynical Westervelt taunts Coverdale in terms that might have been addressed to Bunthorne by the Colonel of Heavy Dragoons: " '. . . you, sir, are probably one of the aesthetic —or shall I rather say ecstatic?—laborers, who have planted themselves hereabouts. This is your forest of Arden; and you are either the banished Duke in person, or one of the chief nobles in his train.' "

Blithedale, then, has something of the Arcadian pastoral about it, and the comparison occurs often enough to bear some weight. The implications are multiple and complex, as elsewhere in Hawthorne. Clearly there adheres to the pastoral scene a taint of mannered artificiality

and absurdity. Yet against this must be balanced the fact
that the imputation is made chiefly by outsiders, hostile,
sympathetic, and merely curious, but in no case knowl-
edgeable. Arcadia suggests an impossible dream; but behind it lies a dignity and a psychological reality backed
by the whole history of the human mind. Blithedale pales
by comparison with the tragic action but softens it, too,
and lends it, as Hawthorne remarks in his preface, a
beauty and attraction of distance. The music, masquerades, and theatricals which occupy the colonists' leisure
hours reinforce the impression of Arcadian make-believe,
but nonetheless they furnish pastime which is unusually
civilized and pure. Nor must we neglect the earnestness
of purpose with which Hawthorne successfully endows
the colonists. These are not courtiers at play, though
Zenobia sometimes manages to suggest Marie Antoinette
in her dairy. The experimenters are seriously pursuing
the ideal life calculated to satisfy most fully the varied
requirements of man. Like Thoreau, they seek to reunite
the spirit and the body, which have long been separated
by the distortions of civilization. They rise above natural
or artificial primitivism by their fullness of vision. This
Arcadianism is truly ideal and imparts its simple dignity
to the central tragedy. On his first departure from Blithedale, Coverdale criticizes its inherent unreality:

I was beginning to lose the sense of what kind of a world
it was, among innumerable schemes of what it might or
ought to be. It was impossible, situated as we were, not to
imbibe the idea that everything in nature and human existence was fluid, or fast becoming so; that the crust of the
earth in many places was broken, and its whole surface por-
tentously upheaving; that it was a day of crisis, and that we

ourselves were in the critical vortex. Our great globe floated in the atmosphere of infinite space like an unsubstantial bubble.

This is one side of the question. The other is succinctly put in Coverdale's conclusion. "More and more I feel that we had struck upon what ought to be a truth."

So much for Blithedale, a setting which is almost an action in itself. The tragic plot is best approached through character; and it is natural to commence with Zenobia, the tragic heroine. As such she is thoroughly orthodox. Her fault is *hubris*; she "had as much native pride as any queen would have known what to do with." She habitually demands of life more than it is able to give; and for this she eventually pays the penalty. She is literally a little larger than life, as becomes the tragic protagonist: "Her hand, though very soft, was larger than most women would like to have, though not a whit too large in proportion with the spacious plan of Zenobia's entire development." One might say that she falls because she is perfect and therefore ripe for destruction. Being endowed with every good gift, she herself is better than life and exists on another plane. She is too vivid, too brilliant, too clearly outlined for the gray half tones of actuality. Thus richly endowed, in her pride she fails to sacrifice to the infernal gods, who love humility in men.

Zenobia's original error, the source of her ultimate destruction, was her union with Westervelt, an entanglement parallel to Miriam's in *The Marble Faun*. This error is allegorically the failure of the unaided intellect to penetrate appearances, for Westervelt is miraculously handsome but completely heartless—a sheer illusion. In this error she follows the pattern of her father Faunt-

173

leroy, who made the same mistake. Fauntleroy, confusing the shadow for the substance, committed a crime in order to continue a life of "external splendor, wherewith he glittered in the eyes of the world, and had no other life than upon this gaudy surface." Zenobia's original error, however, must not be thought to control her subsequent course entirely. Hawthorne does not deny his characters, though they may be deeply entangled, some opportunity of moral escape. In *The House of the Seven Gables* every generation is permitted an awareness of the issues and a clear choice of actions. The chances could hardly be called even, but they nevertheless exist. Zenobia in *The Blithedale Romance* is tested by two moral touchstones, and she fails with both. One, the more important, is her treatment of the tender and sensitive Priscilla; the other is her attitude toward the Blithedale experiment. Both are good but vulnerable, and need kindly care to be preserved.

Priscilla is deliberately sent to Zenobia to be cherished, though Zenobia is not aware that this is part of her test. To assume such responsibility requires an unselfishness and self-restraint which Zenobia does not show. A beautiful, brilliant, and experienced woman, she is merely bored by the adoration of a naïve and defenseless girl of no particular gifts or breeding. The significance of Zenobia's moral failure is intensified when we remark that Priscilla is a symbol of the heart. Zenobia, no doubt, is motivated by jealousy, since the simple Priscilla is preferred to her by Hollingsworth.

At their first meeting Priscilla's appeal is ignored. ". . . she dropped down upon her knees, clasped her hands, and gazed piteously into Zenobia's face. Meeting no kindly reception, her head fell on her bosom." The narrator comments, "I never thoroughly forgave Zenobia for her conduct on this occasion." A little later she applies to Priscilla, in answer to some romantic speculations by Coverdale, a blighting rationalism which comes without love from the analytical intellect. The mysterious girl, says Zenobia, is neither more nor less than a seamstress from the city:

"There is no proof which you would be likely to appreciate, except the needle-marks on the tip of her forefinger. Then, my supposition perfectly accounts for her paleness, her nervousness, and her wretched fragility. Poor thing! She has been stifled with the heat of a salamander-stove, in a small, close room, and has drunk coffee, and fed upon doughnuts, raisins, candy, and all such trash, till she is scarcely half alive; and so, as she has hardly any physique, a poet, like Mr. Miles Coverdale, may be allowed to think her spiritual."

Within its limits this account is true, but it is less than a half-truth, and its cruelty is accented by the fact that Priscilla overhears it and is deeply wounded.

Further acquaintance with Priscilla causes Zenobia to relent, but there is always some mockery and even malice in her later kindliness. Again, jealousy plays some part here. She decks the girl with a sylvan wreath. "Nevertheless, among those fragrant blossoms, conspicuously, too, had been stuck a weed of evil odor and ugly aspect, which, as soon as I detected it, destroyed the effect of all the rest." In a scene purposely arranged to show their mutual fondness she rejects Priscilla as at their first meeting. "But either the girl held her too long, or her fondness was resented as too great a freedom; for Zenobia suddenly put Priscilla decidedly away, and gave her a

haughty look, as from a mistress to a dependant. Old
Moodie shook his head; and again and again I saw him
shake it, as he withdrew along the road; and, at the last
point whence the farm-house was visible, he turned and
shook his uplifted staff." "Old Moodie" happens to be
Fauntleroy, the father of both girls, though at this point
in the story it is not known; and his evident condemnation of Zenobia bears some weight.

Her greatest fault, however, is in returning Priscilla
to the influence of the mesmerist Westervelt, who has
previously capitalized upon the latter's gifts as a medium
by exhibiting her as "The Veiled Lady." Zenobia aban-
dons her to him, very reluctantly indeed, but with full
knowledge of the harm that is likely to follow. To this
injury she adds insult by telling the interpolated story
of "The Veiled Lady," a refinement of cruelty which
becomes outrage at its conclusion, when she suddenly casts
a veil over the hapless Priscilla's head. To these offenses
she further adds an unruffled and mocking hypocrisy:
" 'Ah, the dear little soul! Why, she is really going to
faint! Mr. Coverdale, Mr. Coverdale, pray bring a glass
of water!' "

Zenobia also fails in her treatment of Blithedale. Like
Priscilla, Blithedale is defenseless and needs better than
a fair estimate to show its real value. Zenobia applies to
it the same mocking rationalism as to Priscilla, whereas
both are to be seen most clearly by the eye of faith. She
is overinclined to hit at its Arcadianism. Her criticism is
often legitimate but passes into a skepticism which under
the circumstances is bad faith. Coverdale finds himself
irritated by her "self-complacent, condescending, qualified approval and criticism of a system to which many
individuals—perhaps as highly endowed as our gorgeous

Zenobia—had contributed their all of earthly endeavor, and their loftiest aspirations."

Zenobia is also a test of the Blithedale experiment. It pales before her passionate vitality. Her influence is somewhat ambiguous; her personal force may be unintentionally blighting. Zenobia wears always a magnificent exotic flower, a fitting symbol for her. Seeing her cast one of these blooms aside, the narrator remarks, "The action seemed proper to her character, although, methought, it would still more have fitted the bounteous nature of this beautiful woman to scatter fresh flowers from her hand, and to revive faded ones by her touch." Meditating upon the tiny incident, he continues, "Nevertheless, it was a singular but irresistible effect; the presence of Zenobia caused our heroic enterprise to show like an illusion, a masquerade, a pastoral, a counterfeit Arcadia, in which we grown-up men and women were making a play-day of the years that were given us to live in." This test is genuine; yet allegorically Zenobia represents the rational mind, penetrating but incomplete.

Zenobia is a true tragic character in her magnificence; she is tragic also in her disproportionately heavy punishment. " 'It is genuine tragedy, is it not?' " says she. " 'And you are willing to allow, perhaps, that I have had hard measure.' " It is consistent that her earthly judgment is passed by Hollingsworth, who is no proper arbiter of her true worth. The problem of her guilt is complicated by the question, how strong is Westervelt, her original undoer? Hawthorne endows him with a power which at times makes it appear impossible that she could have escaped him. If it were necessary to account for Zenobia in a word, we should say that "excess" defines her and the reasons for her failure. She is a creature of extremes, whose eyes flash lightning and whose warmth is withering. She is a powerful force which, finding no genuinely worthy opponent, destroys itself by its own momentum.

Hollingsworth, Zenobia's tragic antithesis, is a great spirit perverted by the failure of his mind to direct his heart. His fault is, in brief, lack of self-knowledge; innately a man of the heart, he is led astray by the head and either neglects or misuses his real talents. He is a study in disproportion. In devoting himself exclusively to the "cold, spectral monster" of his philanthropic project of reclaiming criminals, he has violated the truth of his individual human relationships through lack of education and judgment.

... he had taught his benevolence to pour its warm tide exclusively through one channel; so that there was nothing to spare for other great manifestations of love to man, nor scarcely for the nutriment of individual attachments, unless they could minister, in some way, to the terrible egotism which he mistook for an angel of God. Had Hollingsworth's education been more enlarged, he might not so inevitably have stumbled into this pitfall.

Hollingsworth is by nature an elemental creature of the heart, powerful, barrel-chested, shaggy-headed, deep-browed and dark-complexioned: a troglodyte from the heart's caverns, where all is shadow and fire. It is significant that he was once a blacksmith, for in Hawthorne the blacksmith is generally a man of honest and simple strength, with the power of common humanity. Through the symbols of his calling he is related to honest but ill-formed Vulcan, an honorable workman who deals in the

realities of hard metals, which he hammers out forth-
rightly. The blacksmith's forge fire, however, may become hell fire with too much blowing; in the foul caverns of the perverted heart there are potentialities for
brutishness.

Hollingsworth's true gift is for tenderness: ". . . in
his gentler moods, there was a tenderness in his voice,
eyes, mouth, in his gesture, and in every indescribable
manifestation, which few men could resist, and no wom-
en." For the sick Coverdale he is an admirable nurse;
his "more than brotherly attendance" gives "inexpress-
ible comfort." The imagery of the fire and the cave is
employed, by the way, to describe his kind and solicitous
glance. "There never was any blaze of a fireside that
warmed and cheered me, in the down-sinkings and shiv-
erings of my spirit, so effectually as did the light out of
those eyes, which lay so deep and dark under his shaggy
brows." Hollingsworth is the champion of the fragile
Priscilla, whose true worth, invisible to Zenobia, is revealed to him through the intuitive vision of his heart.
In his treatment of Priscilla, "Such casual circumstances
as were here involved would quicken his divine power
of sympathy, and make him seem, while their influence
lasted, the tenderest man and the truest friend on earth."

However, Hollingsworth is by his own avowal committed to inflexible severity. " 'Mortal man has no right
to be so inflexible as it is my nature and necessity to be.' "
His overruling purpose causes in him "a stern and dreadful peculiarity . . . such as could not prove otherwise than
pernicious to the happiness of those who should be drawn
into too intimate a connection with him." His very conviction of the virtue of his plan betrays him into a ghastly

' egotism. It is an idol which appears to him "only benignity and love," but is actually "a spectrum of the very
priest himself, projected upon the surrounding darkness." Seeing him from this point of view, Coverdale
finds him positively devilish—a distortion which corresponds to the inner distortion of Hollingsworth's spirit.

> . . . the features grew more sternly prominent than the
> reality, duskier in their depth and shadow, and more lurid
> in their light; the frown, that had merely flitted across his
> brow, seemed to have contorted it with an adamantine
> wrinkle. On meeting him again, I was often filled with re-
> morse, when his deep eyes beamed kindly upon me, as with
> the glow of a household fire that was burning in a cave.

Here again are the fire and the cave, seen at once in both
aspects. The warm glow of the household fire needs only
a slight intensification to become a lurid gleam from
the Pit.

In his mistaken philanthropy Hollingsworth sins
against Blithedale, against Zenobia, against Coverdale,
and even against Priscilla. He joins the Blithedale experiment without interest in its aims and plans deliberately to betray it for his own purposes. He intends to take
over its grounds for his project of reforming the wicked.
He casts aside Coverdale, his good companion, for refusing to submit himself to the great plan. " 'Be with me,'
said Hollingsworth, 'or be against me! There is no third
choice for you.' " Zenobia, in her final strong counter-
attack against his judgment of her, charges, " '. . . because Coverdale could not be quite your slave, you threw
him ruthlessly away.'" To further his purposes he is ready
to abandon Priscilla to Westervelt and Zenobia, an act

which would have meant her spiritual ruin. However, he recalls the act in time. He uses Zenobia, exploits her love for him, then judges her overharshly and drives her to suicide. All this he does from the most philanthropic motives. Called to account, he is honestly unconscious of fault. " 'With what, then, do you charge me!' asked Hollingsworth, aghast, and greatly disturbed by this attack. 'Show me one selfish end, in all I ever aimed at, and you may cut it out of my bosom with a knife!' " Ironically, he tries to dismiss the indictment as a woman's, governed only by the heart—his own proper sphere— and is properly crushed by Zenobia's last rejoinder, " '. . . a great and rich heart has been ruined in your breast.' "

Hollingsworth is saved, but only by doing lifelong penance for causing Zenobia's death. Himself the criminal, he can no longer spare the time to reform others. His salvation is Priscilla, an emblem of the heart, a part —and the better part—of his own nature. We see him last in an allegorical tableau, walking with Priscilla in a secluded lane:

As they approached me, I observed in Hollingsworth's face a depressed and melancholy look, that seemed habitual; the powerfully built man showed a self-distrustful weakness, and a childlike or childish tendency to press close, and closer still, to the side of the slender woman whose arm was within his. In Priscilla's manner there was a protective and watchful quality, as if she felt herself the guardian of her companion. . . .

Hollingsworth, then, has given over all pride of intellect and all claim to action and lives by the heart alone. The conclusion is not wholly allegorical, for Priscilla is not wholly the heart personified; she is even less completely the heart of Hollingsworth. The reflection bears upon what we have termed his salvation. His own heart is irremediably flawed, and he lives through the spirit and the vision of another. "Salvation," then, is perhaps too confident a word; we can say only that Hollingsworth has made the best recovery possible to him. Whether that is enough must remain, as elsewhere in Hawthorne, an open question. Coverdale's final comment is not cheering: "I see in Hollingsworth an exemplification of the most awful truth in Bunyan's book of such,—from the very gate of heaven there is a by-way to the pit!"

Miles Coverdale, who tells the story, is a complex and interesting figure. It has always been suspected that he is a self-portrait of Hawthorne. In any simple sense he is not, but he is concerned with a number of problems with which Hawthorne was also preoccupied. The chief difficulty in analyzing him, a difficulty which extends from him to *The Blithedale Romance* itself, is a certain skeptical indecision. Coverdale is a man of great potential qualities which are not fulfilled. He remains a self-confessed dilettante who is unable to enter life's main currents. This picture of himself is reflected by the other characters: by Zenobia, who suspects him of being coldly curious, by Hollingsworth, who thinks he wastes his gifts, and by Priscilla, who will not fully trust him. His sense of frustration tinges the book, since he is the interpreter of its action.

We can describe his shortcomings from several points of view. In the first place, he is sufficiently like Hawthorne to be taxed by Hawthorne's habitual self-depreciation. He blames himself over-much for laziness and self-indulgence: he is too conscious of his comfortable bachelor apartments and his pleasure in good wine. Further, as a minor poet he is made faintly ridiculous, which seems unnecessary. A minor poet need not be a trifler, and Coverdale is too much on the defensive about his calling. Hawthorne's conception of poetry is at fault here. It is possible that Coverdale is a typically *modern* poet, whose real seriousness must be veiled with a mocking skepticism. Moreover, the perpetual, hampering Puritan distrust of art should be taken into account. The suspicion that art is after all unfit for serious men is an element in Hawthorne's own excessive modesty, and it touches Coverdale.

We need not consider the faults of Coverdale to be faults of portraiture. He is a study in the spiritual dangers of psychological analysis. As spectator to a tragic drama he is a psychological detective who runs the risk of becoming dehumanized by subjecting other human beings to a coldly scientific curiosity. This danger he escapes, since his interest is at bottom human and loving. As will be seen, he has a stake in the game himself. "Had I been as cold-hearted as I sometimes thought myself, nothing would have interested me more than to witness the play of passions that must thus have been evolved. But, in honest truth, I would really have gone far to save Priscilla, at least, from the catastrophe in which such a drama would be apt to terminate."

Coverdale is the study of a man doomed, not apparently through his own fault, never to live fully. With all the capabilities for living, he remains unawakened and outside. If the comparison is not ridiculous, he is a male Sleeping Beauty whose spell is never broken. Thinking of his own life, Hawthorne says in a well-known letter, "Indeed, we are but shadows—we are not endowed with real life, and all that seems most real about us but the thinnest substance of a dream—till the heart is touched. That touch creates us—then we begin to be—thereby we are beings of reality, and inheritors of eternity." Coverdale's love of Priscilla preserves him from being utterly an outcast; but his love is not returned, and his heart and imagination are never fully aroused. Basically he remains a spectator despite himself.

The role of spectator is made necessary by Coverdale's technical function as narrator and interpreter. Hawthorne does not employ the narrative in the first person elsewhere in his novels, and the use of it here causes special complications. As the previous interpretations have consistently emphasized, Hawthorne's point of view is generally objective and balanced, often to the point of ambiguity. To reconcile this objectivity with the subjective perceptions of a single character is not easy, and Hawthorne increases the difficulty of his problem by permitting Coverdale a relatively large part in the story, while as narrator and chorus he cannot really participate in or materially affect the movement of the plot. Thus Coverdale is always on the verge of action, yet never acting, in a kind of rhythmic hesitation. At the beginning of the book he is almost given the responsibility for Priscilla's welfare at Blithedale, but the charge is withdrawn from him. Zenobia nearly confides in him but draws back. In love with Priscilla, Coverdale cannot feel that he has the right to intervene for her; this right is given instead to Hollingsworth, to whom, although superior in intellect and sensitivity, Coverdale remains subsidiary. Since Hawthorne has chosen to place him in the forefront, Coverdale is forced to maintain a delicate balance between spectator and participant which must not be upset. When this balance is upset by his direct avowal in the last chapter of his love for Priscilla, the result is unfortunate. The tension of his attitude, an important element of the tone of the book, is here relaxed and dissipated.

His function as chorus completes the definition of his role:

My own part in these transactions was singularly subordinate. It resembled that of the Chorus in a classic play, which seems to be set aloof from the possibility of personal concernment, and bestows the whole measure of its hope or fear, its exultation or sorrow, on the fortunes of others, between whom and itself this sympathy is the only bond. Destiny, it may be,—the most skilful of stage-managers,—seldom chooses to arrange its scenes, and carry forward its drama, without securing the presence of at least one calm observer. It is his office to give applause when due, and sometimes an inevitable tear, to detect the final fitness of incident to character, and distil in his long-brooding thought the whole morality of the performance.

Coverdale's interpretation is final. We receive the meaning of the action through him. This superiority, even infallibility, places him on a separate plane, and his different status must be disguised by giving him defects and disproportions. Thus his superior intelligence is balanced by a fastidiousness and hesitation which make him apparently ineffectual but preserve his role as the ideal spectator. Once, at least, his insight renders him the inner voice of conscience itself, which yet speaks from without. This occasion is his merciless interrogation of Hollingsworth at their final meeting.

"I have come, Hollingsworth," said I, "to view your grand edifice for the reformation of criminals. Is it finished yet?"

"No, nor begun," answered he, without raising his eyes. "A very small one answers all my purposes. . . ."

"Up to this moment," I inquired, "how many criminals have you reformed?"

"Not one," said Hollingsworth, with his eyes still fixed on the ground. "Ever since we parted, I have been busy with a single murderer."

Coverdale is a modern poet and moralist who hides his real emotions in cynicism. Westervelt (Western World?), the source of the original ill, represents spiritual evil in its most characteristic modern guise. He is wholly a materialist, a living negation of all values. He believes neither in good nor in evil, as is evident in his feelings about Zenobia's suicide. To him her act is a meaningless waste for which he himself takes no blame. " 'It was an idle thing—a foolish thing—for Zenobia to do,' said he. 'She was the last woman in the world to whom death could have been necessary. It was too absurd! I have no patience with her.' " Westervelt possesses the enormous strength of imperviousness, linked with great practical intelligence. The native passion of the forceful Zenobia is utterly wasted upon him. "As for Westervelt, he was not a whit more warmed by Zenobia's passion than a salamander by the heat of its native furnace. He would have been absolutely statuesque, save for a look of slight perplexity, tinctured strongly with derision."

The main principle of Westervelt's character is the materialist error of mistaking appearance for reality; like

Judge Pyncheon, he sees only "the big, solid unrealities" of life. He is not only the victim of this delusion, but the cause of it in others. Zenobia was originally entrapped by his amazing physical beauty; she found nothing beneath the surface. His real falsity and deadness is quickly apparent to Coverdale and is only accentuated by his faultless exterior. This quality of sham is prosaically symbolized by one false note; on close inspection it is discovered that his handsome teeth are false. In his capacity as mesmerist he commits the Unpardonable Sin, like Ethan Brand, by violating the individuality of Priscilla; but unlike Brand he is quite unconscious of it. Whereas Brand is a man of immense although warped insight, Westervelt is turned completely away from truth. Westervelt, in contrast to the fiery Brand, sins by negation.

This contrast of appearance-reality is primary in Westervelt, but there is a malign intelligence still deeper beneath his cool nullity. Westervelt is Satan walking the modern world. As walking stick he carries the serpent staff, which in "Young Goodman Brown" betrays the devil's presence. At times his eyes sparkle "as if the Devil were peeping out of them." Somehow, in fact, the cold skepticism of the modern materialist leads to the fires of the Pit. Man cannot banish the spirit; Westervelt has depths which must be filled and cannot be long ignored. Left void, hell rushes into him to usurp the place of its betters. He attempts to do without good and evil, and is damned for his error.

Priscilla, whom Westervelt almost ruins, is allegorically the heart miraculously untouched by sin. She is at once powerful and vulnerable, a paradox which is epitomized in the shimmering garment of the Veiled Lady. It is evanescent and luminous; it insulates her from the world and yet suggests a sensitive spirit. The dissatisfaction which one must feel towards her character comes from a simplicity which goes beyond verisimilitude, like the figure of Hilda in *The Marble Faun*, whom she resembles. As the pure heart, she is a moral touchstone. Westervelt tries to exploit her, and Zenobia is incapable of seeing her value. The heart of Hollingsworth intuitively perceives its like, but he comes near to betraying her nonetheless. Coverdale's love, Priscilla does not encourage and perhaps does not even imagine. This may be taken as an indictment of Coverdale, but it could conceivably be an indictment of Priscilla instead. Coverdale is the most complex character in the book, Priscilla the simplest, and our final verdict need not be undividedly in favor of simplicity.

Priscilla is also a symbol of faith, which pierces intuitively to spiritual truth. In this respect she is closer to various children in Hawthorne's fiction than to any other adult. She is like little Joe in "Ethan Brand," Ilbrahim of "The Gentle Boy," and the sympathetic child of "The Chimaera" in *A Wonder Book*, who alone comprehends the aspirations of Bellerophon. This child later becomes "a mighty poet" and masters the winged horse Pegasus more fully than did Bellerophon himself. But Priscilla represents faith objectively as well, and one must be able to imagine in order to appreciate her. Thus Coverdale and Hollingsworth are superior to the materialistic skeptics of the book, Zenobia and Westervelt. As faith, Priscilla is also an embodiment of the sympathetic romantic imagination, marvellously sensitive and penetrating, but in this instance unsupported by judgment and experience and therefore insecure and dangerously exposed to evil. Priscilla is almost completely passive; she is controlled by others, and her welfare is at the mercy of their decisions. That she escapes her pitfalls indicates that goodness and trust awake their counterparts in others; but she runs many dangers.

Priscilla will lead us to a consideration of the special atmosphere and tone of *The Blithedale Romance*, a question which has been hinted at in discussing Coverdale. Hawthorne is dealing with contemporary life, and he has the problem of wresting from its confusion and phenomenal chaos the kind of design and meaning which alone interest him. In other novels he escapes through the past, or, as in *The Marble Faun,* through a setting remote from everyday America. Blithedale itself, as he says in his preface, is a distancing device, but the book remains close to the actual and the present. He is, then, more on the defensive than elsewhere and is more conscious of the difficulty of cracking the brute surface of things to get at the deep core of meaning. This, I think, explains the skepticisms and the frustrations of Coverdale and the less confident and reposeful tone of the story. It perhaps also explains why the primary issues of *The Blithedale Romance* are between skepticism and faith, materialism and idealism—issues not to be found in the other novels.

# XIII

## *The Marble Faun*

THE CRUCIAL PROBLEM of *The Marble Faun* is far-reaching in its implications. Has the faun Donatello been ruined or ennobled by his human crime? Miriam, the comrade of his fall, succinctly states the issue and its broadest relationship:

"The story of the fall of man! Is it not repeated in our romance of Monte Beni? And may we follow the analogy yet further? Was that very sin,—into which Adam precipitated himself and all his race,—was it the destined means by which, over a long pathway of toil and sorrow, we are to attain a higher, brighter, and profounder happiness, than our lost birthright gave? Will not this idea account for the permitted existence of sin, as no other theory can?"

From this perilous moral the sculptor Kenyon, who may with some caution be taken as speaking for Hawthorne, recoils. " 'It is too dangerous, Miriam! I cannot follow you!' . . . 'Mortal man has no right to tread on the ground where you now set your feet.' " Nevertheless, we find him a few pages later advancing the same idea to the innocent Hilda:

"Here comes my perplexity," continued Kenyon. "Sin has educated Donatello, and elevated him. Is sin, then,—

which we deem such a dreadful blackness in the universe,—
is it, like sorrow, merely an element of human education,
through which we struggle to a higher and purer state than
we could otherwise have attained? Did Adam fall, that we
might ultimately rise to a far loftier paradise than his?"

Hilda repudiates the notion with horror. The pattern
of advance and retreat is the same in both instances. Most
commentators on *The Marble Faun*, however, have accepted the speculation itself, rather than the withdrawal,
as representing Hawthorne's true intention. This interpretation leaves us with the doctrine of "the fortunate
fall," according to which man's sin and expulsion from
Eden is in reality a proof of God's mercy and concealed
benevolence. On the other hand Austin Warren, in his
excellent introduction to his selections from Hawthorne,
argues stoutly for the opposite view. Hawthorne, he
maintains, is orthodox (Calvinistically orthodox, that is)
in his thinking about human nature and himself retreats
from and rejects the full possibilities of his speculation.
Mr. Warren's opinion is the sounder of the two and is
very cogently presented. Yet he errs in presuming that
in the fictional substance of *The Marble Faun* the choice
is made at all. Rather, it is only offered. Hawthorne neither accepts nor rejects; it is not his habit to come to ultimate conclusions. In the body of his works there are too
many references to "the fortunate fall" to dismiss the
idea with safety, while there are none which, read in context, would enable us to accept it as a doctrine. He leaves
the question in suspension, which in *The Marble Faun*
becomes the central mystery of man.

The suspension between opposite beliefs is the life-
principle of *The Marble Faun*, embodied in imagery

and symbolism, in character, in setting, and in movement or progression. I shall have most to say about the figurative patterns of imagery and symbol. The central suspension of *The Marble Faun* is an opposition between simplicity and complexity, which rests deliberately unresolved at the end. Simplicity is Donatello the faun in his original innocence, complexity is Donatello humanized, matured, and saddened. Simplicity is the Golden Age, the Arcadia which is the Faun's proper setting; complexity is the nineteenth century in which he is misplaced. Simplicity is the rural life of Tuscany, whence Donatello comes; complexity is Rome, the greatest of cities, where he meets with love and sin. Simplicity is Eden before the serpent and the flaming sword; complexity is the wide world of the exile, the real world of Hawthorne's characters. Simplicity is heaven itself (which will cause us most difficulty); complexity is human earth. Simplicity is, in fact, either sub- or super-human, while complexity is the stuff of humanity.

The simplicity of Donatello is that of a subhuman being, who is yet capable of virtues which humans have not. In his prototype the Faun of Praxiteles "the characteristics of the brute creation meet and combine with those of humanity." The peculiar virtue of this creature for Hawthorne is stated concisely at the end of Chapter I. "And after all, the idea may have been no dream, but rather a poet's reminiscence of a period when man's affinity with nature was more strict, and his fellowship with every living thing more intimate and dear." The value of this affinity and fellowship will be apparent to those who are familiar with Hawthorne's dread of spiritual isolation and his corresponding emphasis upon the social bond of mankind.

Donatello's family of Monte Beni is of ancient, even legendary descent, its line disappearing in prehistoric mists, before Rome, before the Etruscans, into the fabulous Golden Age itself. The legendary progenitor of this family "was a being not altogether human, yet partaking so largely of the gentlest human qualities, as to be neither awful nor shocking to the imagination." Married to a human maiden, from him

sprang a vigorous progeny that took its place unquestioned among human families. In that age, however, and long afterwards, it showed the ineffaceable lineaments of its wild paternity: it was a pleasant and kindly race of men, but capable of savage fierceness, and never quite restrainable within the trammels of social law. They were strong, active, genial, cheerful as the sunshine, passionate as the tornado. Their lives were rendered blissful by an unsought harmony with nature.

In the course of time the family lost most of its original qualities, but about once in a century a son would appear who reproduced its ancient character afresh (as the original Colonel Pyncheon kept recurring at intervals in the Pyncheon family of *The House of the Seven Gables*). Donatello, the last of the race, is such an atavism. The typical Monte Beni is thus described:

Beautiful, strong, brave, kindly, sincere, of honest impulses, and endowed with simple tastes and the love of homely pleasures, he was believed to possess gifts by which he could associate himself with the wild things of the forests, and with the fowls of the air, and could feel a sympathy even with the trees, among which it was his joy to dwell. On the other hand, there were deficiencies both of intellect and heart, and especially, as it seemed, in the development of the higher portion of man's nature. These defects were less perceptible in early youth, but showed themselves more strongly with advancing age, when, as the animal spirits settled down upon a lower level, the representative of the Monte Beni was apt to become sensual, addicted to gross pleasures, heavy, unsympathizing, and insulated within the narrow limits of a surly selfishness.

The Faun of Monte Beni, it appears, is both more and less than human in his simplicity. The fit setting for this creature is the Golden Age, or Arcadia, to which there are more than twenty explicit references in *The Marble Faun*. At one point the two are distinguished ("It was a glimpse far back into Arcadian life, or further still, into the Golden Age. . . ."), but they are generally equivalent. The peasants of Monte Beni represent the closest actual approach to Arcadian life, and these recognize in Donatello a being more primitive and closer to nature than themselves. The remainder of the quotation can be used to show further the mingled virtues and defects of such a state: ". . . before mankind was burdened with sin and sorrow, and before pleasure had been darkened with those shadows that bring it into high relief, and make it happiness."

" '. . . no Faun in Arcadia was ever a greater simpleton than Donatello,' " says Miriam in the opening chapter. Somewhat later she remarks, " '. . . the world is sadly changed nowadays; grievously changed, poor Donatello, since those happy times when your race used to dwell in the Arcadian woods. . . . You have reappeared on earth some centuries too late.' " The grounds of the Villa

Borghese are "those Arcadian woods," in which Donatello appears in his element. Here he professes his love to the subtle and sophisticated Miriam: ". . . on her part, —such was the contagion of his simplicity,—Miriam heard it without anger or disturbance, though with no responding emotion. It was as if they had strayed across the limits of Arcadia. . . ." On this same occasion an impromptu dance strikes up in which all within hearing take part, aroused chiefly by the "indescribable potency" of the music Donatello elicits from a tambourine. "Here, as it seemed, had the Golden Age come back again within the precincts of this sunny glade, thawing mankind out of their cold formalities, releasing them from irksome restraint. . . ." One might quote at much greater length to the same effect, but these references are sufficient to indicate the power of the Golden Age and Arcadian myths upon Hawthorne's imagination.

This value of simplicity is neither dismissed nor supplanted in *The Marble Faun;* manifestly incomplete, it yet remains with an enchantment never dimmed. Donatello is humanized and refined, but with real loss. Hawthorne twice suggests the place of this happy innocence in a state of ideal perfection, but the hinted synthesis is a perfection not of earth. " 'Nature needed, and still needs, this beautiful creature,' " says the sculptor Kenyon, " 'standing betwixt man and animal, sympathizing with each. . . .' " Again, with reference to the vexed question of Donatello's hidden ears, it is remarked, ". . . into what regions of rich mystery would it extend Donatello's sympathies, to be thus linked (and by no monstrous chain) with what we call the inferior tribes of being, whose simplicity, mingled with his human intelligence, might partly restore what man has lost of the divine!"

195

Linked with the simplicity of Arcadia and the Golden Age is the simplicity of Eden before the Fall. The Borghese garden "is like Eden in its loveliness; like Eden, too, in the fatal spell [in this instance malaria] that removes it beyond the scope of man's actual possessions." Kenyon finds Edenlike the groves of Monte Beni, with an added charm from his fallen vision:

The sculptor strayed amid its vineyards and orchards, its dells and tangled shrubberies, with somewhat the sensations of an adventurer who should find his way to the site of an ancient Eden, and behold its loveliness through the transparency of that gloom which has been brooding over those haunts of innocence ever since the fall. Adam saw it in a brighter sunshine, but never knew the shade of pensive beauty which Eden won from his expulsion.

Eden is the Christian counterpart of the pagan Golden Age. Hawthorne does not venture to identify the two, Eden having always a special sanctity, but in *The Marble Faun* they are clearly copresent, simplicities of similar import. Eden occurs far less in direct reference than do the Golden Age and Arcadia, but the story of the Fall is pervasive throughout.

The final and most difficult emblem of simplicity is heaven itself, in *The Marble Faun* most frequently embodied in the character of Hilda, the dove. It is the most difficult symbol since it cannot be distinguished from the lower simplicities of Eden and the Golden Age. They are beginnings; heaven is a culmination. They represent a term of the problem, a pole to be reconciled with its opposite; heaven should be solution and reconcilement. In Eden and the Age of Gold complexity has not yet appeared. The simplicity of heaven should include and resolve complexity. Yet it does not.

This problem is to be found not only in Hawthorne and *The Marble Faun*, but universally. It is a characteristically but not solely Christian problem. Heaven, which should be the resolution of complexity, appears instead to fall back upon avoidance and negation. For most imaginations the dilemma is, "Who wants to play on a harp, anyway?" Beatitude is difficult to envision. We know that Milton's hell is more impressive than his heaven, that the *Inferno* outweighs the *Paradiso*, and that Mr. Eliot evokes his Wasteland more convincingly than he escapes from it. In literature the problem is to achieve Plato's unmixed virtue without sacrificing probability. Most of us, I presume, would side with Aristotle, who prefers the faulty Achilles of the *Iliad*.

This consideration returns us to the character of Hilda as a symbol for heaven, which unquestionably she is. She lives among doves in a tower, a Christian vestal virgin tending an eternal flame. She is seen most typically robed in white, the white of simplicity and innocence. Her proper atmosphere is her tower room above the streets of ancient, human, sinful Rome: "Only the domes of churches ascend into this airy region, and hold up their golden crosses on a level with her eye. . . ." She has a "perfect simplicity." She lives amid "pure thoughts and innocent enthusiasms." A finely gifted copyist of painting, her closest affinity is with Fra Angelico, her favorite picture Guido's unruffled Michael slaying an inadequate dragon. Transfigured with sudden happiness, she "suggests how angels come by their beauty." Kenyon compares her to a spirit and wishes humbly, and with some sense of impiety, " 'that I might draw her down to an earthly fireside!' " Amid the evil of Rome she walks untouched:

With respect to whatever was evil, foul, and ugly, in this populous and corrupt city, she trod as if invisible, and not only so, but blind. She was altogether unconscious of anything wicked that went along the same pathway, but without jostling or impeding her, any more than gross substance hinders the wanderings of a spirit. Thus it is, that, bad as the world is said to have grown, innocence continues to make a paradise around itself, and keep it still unfallen.

As representative of heaven's simplicity, she consistently rejects the complex. Despite her gentleness, her moral judgments are relentless. " 'O Hilda,' exclaims Miriam, 'your innocence is like a sharp sword! . . . Your judgments are often terribly severe, though you seem all made up of gentleness and mercy.' " This statement is made before Miriam has exposed herself to her friend's eyes; she has no later cause to change her mind. After her sin and misfortune Miriam feels some bitterness, some sense of unfairness in Hilda's gentle but complete rejection of her. Kenyon's defense of the sinners is totally unacceptable to Hilda, and he charges her with lack of mercy.

" 'Ah, Hilda,' replied Kenyon, 'you do not know, for you could never learn it from your own heart, which is all purity and rectitude, what a mixture of good there may be in things evil.' " She answers, " '. . . there is, I believe, only one right and one wrong; and I do not understand, and may God keep me from ever understanding, how two things so totally unlike can be mistaken for one another. . . .' " To this he concludes, " 'I always felt you, my dear friend, a terribly severe judge, and have been perplexed to conceive how such tender sympathy could coexist with the remorselessness of a steel blade. You need no mercy, and therefore know not how to show any.' " It is interesting to notice the repetition of the metaphor of the sharp sword of innocence. Could it bear a relation to the flaming sword of the expulsion, which occurs several times in *The Marble Faun?*

The simplicity of Hilda is inadequate for a complete judgment of human motives and values; this lack is felt in her by persons themselves not wholly qualified, and yet to be respected. Donatello, saddened and transformed by sin, makes the case against Hilda when Kenyon urges him to view some pictures by Fra Angelico:

"You have shown me some of Fra Angelico's pictures, I remember," answered Donatello; "his angels look as if they had never taken a flight out of heaven; and his saints seem to have been born saints, and always to have lived so. Young maidens, and all innocent persons, I doubt not, may find great delight and profit in looking at such holy pictures. But they are not for me." "Your criticism, I fancy, has great moral depth," replied Kenyon: "and I see in it the reason why Hilda so highly appreciates Fra Angelico's pictures."

Miriam makes the same criticism against Guido's Archangel, a favorite of Hilda's:

"But is it thus that virtue looks the moment after its death-struggle with evil? No, no; I could have told Guido better. A full third of the Archangel's feathers should have been torn from his wings; the rest all ruffled, till they looked like Satan's own! His sword should be streaming with blood, and perhaps broken half-way to the hilt; his armor crushed, his robes rent, his breast gory; a bleeding gash on his brow, cutting right across the stern scowl of battle! He should press his foot hard down upon the old serpent, as if his very soul depended upon it, feeling him squirm mightily, and doubting whether the fight were half over yet, and how the victory might turn!"

While Hilda is the symbol of the simplicity of heaven, we cannot accept her judgment of earthly values, though we cannot finally reject it either. One answer lies in the lack of differentiation between the innocence of Eden and the innocence of heaven. Hilda is a child of Eden, to whom at Miriam's sin "Adam falls anew, and Paradise, heretofore in unfaded bloom, is lost again, and closed forever, with the fiery swords gleaming at its gates." Hilda, however, remains substantially unaltered by her contact with sin, despite her genuine and deep distress. We have seen that she walks amid evil untouched; a child of Eden she remains, bearing with her her paradise.

Another explanation is the inevitable confusion in Hilda of human and superhuman, earth and heaven. To Miriam's plea for understanding and forgiveness she is forced to answer:

"If I were one of God's angels, with a nature incapable of stain, and garments that could never be spotted, I would keep ever at your side, and try to lead you upward. But I am a poor, lonely girl, whom God has set here in an evil world, and given her only a white robe, and bid her wear it back to Him, as white as when she put it on. Your powerful magnetism would be too much for me. The pure, white atmosphere, in which I try to discern what things are good and true, would be discolored."

Miriam rejoins, " 'As an angel, you are not amiss; but, as a human creature, and a woman among earthly men and women, you need a sin to soften you.' " One sees the complication; Hilda is at once human and divine. She is the emblem of heaven, yet her limitation hints faintly at a higher simplicity which embraces all humanity, instead of, like her, rejecting much of life. Hawthorne intends to go no further; engrossed in the idea of divine perfection, he yet draws a line beyond which his speculation does not trespass. Hilda represents for him a real, valuable, and attractive aspect of human life, which also is fortunately tinctured with divinity. He believes that there are such women as she—his own wife, for example —that they are significant and representative, and that they are worthy not only of reverence but of love.

As a literary character Hilda is not wholly unbelievable, but in isolation she fails to satisfy. Her limited perfection makes her inflexible and her actions too predictable. She is justifiable as one among other elements in the balance of a Hawthorne novel. One must feel, however, that Hawthorne was mistaken in making her the center of interest for a long section of the book. (Here one might notice at the same time an apparent design of fairly apportioning the emphasis among the four principal characters.) Hilda cannot act, but is only acted upon, since action is imperfection. One can believe in the spiritual misery arising from her knowledge of the crime of Miriam and Donatello, which drives this "daughter of the Puritans" to confession to a Catholic priest; but one cannot fully sympathize with her. Hilda is too strong in her simplicity for us to accept her dilemma as more than temporary. Likewise we cannot share Kenyon's anxiety at her sudden disappearance, despite Hawthorne's not wholly serious efforts to frighten us with suggestions about the terrible things that can happen to a virgin in Rome. Not to Hilda; we have been convinced of her invulnerability.

Against the simplicities of Donatello, the Golden Age and Arcadia, Eden, heaven, and its saintly Hilda stand the complexities of the present, of Miriam, of modern Rome, of ancient Rome which it evokes, and of the Roman Church. First, the refined but saddened nineteenth century of Kenyon and Miriam are directly opposed to the Golden Age of Donatello and the timeless Eden of Hilda. " 'Pray do not,' " Kenyon advises Donatello, " 'under a notion of improvement, take upon yourself to be sombre, thoughtful, and penitential, like all the rest of us.' " Donatello's old butler finds that " 'the world has grown either too evil, or else too wise and sad, for such men as the old Counts of Monte Beni used to be. His very first taste of it, as you see, has changed and spoilt my poor young lord.' " For Donatello the world is too wise and sad, and, it may be, for Hilda too evil. The world has passed its childhood, and with it much that was good and innocent:

. . . the once genial earth produces, in every successive generation, fewer flowers than used to gladden the preceding ones. Not that the modes and seeming possibilities of human enjoyment are rarer in our refined and softened era,—on the contrary, they never before were nearly so abundant,— but that mankind are getting so far beyond the childhood of their race that they scorn to be happy any longer. A sim-

ple and joyous character can find no place for itself among
the sage and sombre figures that would put his unsophisticated cheerfulness to shame. The entire system of man's
affairs, as at present established, is built up purposely to
exclude the careless and happy soul.

Rome, consummate creation of humanity and time,
possesses both the horror and the fascination of complexity. Rome is the essence of paradox:

We know not how to characterize, in any accordant and
compatible terms, the Rome that lies before us; its sunless
alleys, and streets of palaces; its churches, lined with the
gorgeous marbles that were originally polished for the
adornment of pagan temples; its thousands of evil smells,
mixed up with fragrance of rich incense, diffused from as
many censers; its little life, deriving feeble nutriment from
what has long been dead. Everywhere, some fragment of
ruin suggesting the magnificence of a former epoch; everywhere, moreover, a Cross,—and nastiness at the foot of it.
As the sum of all, there are recollections that kindle the
soul, and a gloom and languor that depress it beyond any
depth of melancholic sentiment that can be elsewhere known.
Yet how is it possible to say an unkind or irreverential
word of Rome? The city of all time, and of all the world!
The spot for which man's great life and deeds have done
so much, and for which decay has done whatever glory and
dominion could not do.

Rome, the human and complex, is the antithesis of
the Arcadian seclusion of Monte Beni's groves. Donatello, it is fancifully said, wilts in the oppressive air of
the city. Its august child, the Roman Catholic Church,

is also a symbol of complexity. It offends against the simplicity of worship, and also from an excess of humanity, since in it the human masquerades as superhuman. Its complex hierarchy and multiplicity of forms contrast directly with the simplicity of Puritan worship in which Hilda was reared. It arouses a complex mixture of affection, reverence, and disgust. Of wayside shrines to the Virgin it is said: "There are many things in the religious customs of these people that seem good; many things, at least, that might be both good and beautiful, if the soul of goodness and the sense of beauty were as much alive in the Italians now as they must have been when those customs were first imagined and adopted." Catholicism "marvellously adapts itself to every human need." It "supplies a multitude of external forms, in which the spiritual may be clothed and manifested." For Hawthorne the abiding flaw is its excessive admixture of the human: "If there were but angels to work it, instead of the very different class of engineers who now manage its cranks and safety-valves, the system would soon vindicate the dignity and holiness of its origin." The Roman Church is fitly symbolized by the gorgeous coloring of a painted window. Kenyon, a devout man in a vaguely Puritan tradition, thus characterizes it:

"Daylight, in its natural state, ought not to be admitted here. It should stream through a brilliant illusion of saints and hierarchies, and old scriptural images, and symbolized dogmas, purple, blue, golden, and a broad flame of scarlet. Then, it would be just such an illumination as the Catholic faith allows to its believers. But give me—to live and die in— the pure, white light of heaven!"

Hilda, a "daughter of the Puritans," is tempted by the advantages of Catholicism and in confessing her secret to a priest receives them in part, but she remains faithful to the "white light" of a simpler and more purely supernatural communion.

Complexity is a human attribute, failing, and endowment. An important element in the complex of human nineteenth-century Rome is the ponderous memory of its ancient ancestor, the apotheosis of the human. Everywhere the "massive old stones and indestructible bricks of imperial Rome" are physically present and spiritually oppressive. The Rome of today "seems like nothing but a heap of broken rubbish, thrown into the great chasm between our own days and the Empire, merely to fill it up." In a significant and constantly recurring image, old Rome "lies like the dead corpse of a giant, decaying for centuries, with no survivor mighty enough even to bury it." The tremendous tombs of the Appian Way are emblems of the doom of human grandeur: "Nothing remains to the dishonored sepulchres, except their massiveness." Its most perfect embodiment is the equestrian statue of Marcus Aurelius on the Capitoline Hill:

A sight of the old heathen emperor is enough to create an evanescent sentiment of loyalty even in a democratic bosom, so august does he look, so fit to rule, so worthy of man's profoundest homage and obedience, so inevitably attractive of his love. He stretches forth his hand with an air of grand beneficence and sunlimited authority, as if uttering a decree from which no appeal was permissible, but in which the obedient subject would find his highest interests consulted; a command that was in itself a benediction.

Human grandeur of character can reach no higher. A still better spiritual force, however, emanates from the "grand benignity" of the statue of Pope Julius in Perugia, which blesses the union of Miriam and Donatello, "stretching out the hand of benediction over . . . this guilty and repentant pair." An emblem of the Church, as Aurelius is of ancient Rome, the pontiff outweighs the emperor through a greater, though still imperfect, admixture of the divine.

The conception of the Renaissance also enters into the treatment of human values. The Renaissance is present in the great Roman palaces and in art, particularly painting. These palaces, like the ruins of the ancients, present an ironic portrait of the vanity of human achievement in their grandeur and squalor, their splendor and lack of comfort. There is, perhaps, an added reproach of perversity, since they were built by Christian cardinals as well as princes, who had better things before their eyes. Similarly, the paintings of the masters have an all-too-human taint. Titian is perhaps the type of the merely human; Raphael, half-divine, mingles his earthly loves with the likenesses of heaven:

And who can trust the religious sentiment of Raphael, or receive any of his Virgins as heaven-descended likenesses, after seeing, for example, the Fornarina of the Barberini Palace, and feeling how sensual the artist must have been to paint such a brazen trollop of his own accord, and lovingly? Would the Blessed Mary reveal herself to his spiritual vision, and favor him with sittings alternately with that type of glowing earthliness, the Fornarina?

Here we run the danger of upsetting Hawthorne's balance. This condemnation occurs in a section which is as a whole a defense of Italian Renaissance painting. The criticism is immediately qualified, and is in any event a dramatic reflection of Hilda's momentary depression of spirit. The indictment remains, however, along with its qualifications.

There is in *The Marble Faun* an "organic" theory of art which extends in its application into all other problems of the book. In every discussion of painting and sculpture the individual work is judged according to the degree in which it possesses a unifying life and light. The meritless work, or the falsely fine, as Flemish genre painting, is empty technique, mere copy, dead mass. In her spiritual misery Hilda

now grew acquainted with that icy demon of weariness, who haunts great picture galleries. He is a plausible Mephistopheles, and possesses the magic that is the destruction of all other magic. He annihilates color, warmth, and, more especially, sentiment and passion, at a touch. If he spare anything, it will be some such matter as an earthen pipkin, or a bunch of herrings by Teniers; a brass kettle, in which you can see your face, by Gerard Douw. . . .

This is the fallacy of art; such painting represents the triumph of opacity—deadness masquerading as life.

In describing Hilda's gifts as a copyist, Hawthorne makes the Coleridgean distinction between *copy* and *imitation*, a distinction parallel to *mechanical* and *organic*. Hilda, by a "guiding light of sympathy," is able to go "straight to the central point, in which the master had conceived his work." She achieves not merely the letter but the spirit of the original. She attains to what Coleridge terms imitation; others achieve a copy only:

Other copyists—if such they are worthy to be called—attempt only a superficial imitation. Copies of the old masters in this sense are produced by thousands; there are artists . . . who spend their lives in painting the works, or perhaps one single work, of one illustrious painter over and over again: thus they convert themselves into Guido machines, or Raphaelic machines. Their performances, it is true, are often wonderfully deceptive to a careless eye; but working entirely from the outside, and seeking only to reproduce the surface, these men are sure to leave out that indefinable nothing, that inestimable something, that constitutes the life and soul through which the picture gets its immortality.

Truly organic art imitates from deep within; it has a life and soul, and thus it is immortal. The notion of organic imitation expressed in *The Marble Faun* is thoroughly Platonic and Christian. Art is always the imperfect imitation of a higher reality. The conception is loftier than the completed work. Thus Hilda is successful because she follows "precisely the same process step by step through which the original painter had trodden to the development of his idea." In Chapter XV, "An Aesthetic Company," rough sketches by the great masters are found more interesting than the paintings for which they are preliminary studies. "There is an effluence of divinity in the first sketch; and there, if anywhere, you find the pure light of inspiration, which the subsequent toil of the artist serves to bring out in stronger lustre, indeed, but likewise adulterates it with what belongs to an inferior mood." Hilda comforts Kenyon, momentarily discouraged over his fine statue of Cleopatra, by reflecting:

". . . this final despair, and sense of shortcoming, must always be the reward and punishment of itself, which you at first mistake for the ethereal reality, but soon find that the latter has escaped out of your closest embrace."

The corresponding defect of art is literal, uninspired imitation. Some sculptors, for example, of mere "mechanical ingenuity," "might have been fitly employed in making wax-work [wax-works, by the way, are one of Coleridge's examples of mechanical copy]. How terrible should be the thought, that the nude woman whom the modern artist patches together, bit by bit, from a dozen heterogeneous models, meaning nothing by her, shall last as long as the Venus of the Capitol!" Great Italian art is at times likely to reveal "a keen intellectual perception, and a marvellous knack of external arrangement, instead of the live sympathy and sentiment. . . ." Thus "a taste for pictorial art is often no more than a polish upon the hard enamel of an artificial character."

This conception of art is paralleled in other topics and fields of imagery. Rome itself, the Roman Church, and various Italian institutions all err in perpetuating mere mass when the life has vanished, so that the dead hand of the past is stiflingly heavy upon the weak human spirit. Forms once pervaded with life now slowly rot untouched and poison existence in their decay. Matter bulks larger than spirit, and the odor of human mortality is everywhere. The recurrent image of ancient Rome as a gigantic, unburied corpse is a case in point; the graveyard of the Capuchin monks in a subterranean crypt beneath their church is a single vivid instance. Skeletons lie everywhere, with skulls, "some quite bare, and others still covered with yellow skin, and hair that has known the earth-damps." The weight of mortality is overpowering:

. . . the cemetery of the Capuchins is no place to nourish celestial hopes; the soul sinks forlorn and wretched under all this burden of dusty death; the holy earth from Jerusalem, so imbued is it with mortality, has grown as barren of the flowers of Paradise as it is of earthly weeds and grass. . . . Not here can we feel ourselves immortal, where the very altars in these chapels of horrible consecration are heaps of human bones.

Now the life which is the value of art and of human institutions clearly comes from heaven. To some extent complexity = humanity = mortality = dead matter in *The Marble Faun,* while simplicity = divinity = immortality = life and light; but once again we must qualify and redress the balance. Art is represented by the Renaissance, not by the Primitives, although Hawthorne is aware of Giotto and Cimabue. The Roman Church is by no means condemned. The humanity of ancient Rome is more powerful still than following ages, and Hawthorne enlists our sympathies with the complex Miriam and against the simple Hilda. If one considers this problem, we may do well before finding Hilda overrighteous to heed the adjuration, "Clear your mind of cant!" How many of us would be willing to condone a particularly terrible murder committed before our eyes? Would we wish to go further than Hilda, who keeps the secret while breaking off relations with the murderers? That the question seldom arises in this light is evidence of Hawthorne's skill in framing the problem and certainly reveals his sympathy with the guilty.

In the symbols of art complexity as well as simplicity may be imbued with life. On the opening page, among the wonders of the Capitol we find a "symbol of the

Human Soul ... in the pretty figure of a child, clasping a dove to her bosom, but assaulted by a snake"—a symbol which fitly preludes the book. Kenyon's sculpture of Cleopatra, the embodiment of human complexity, is a vital masterpiece:

> In a word, all Cleopatra—fierce, voluptuous, passionate, tender, wicked, terrible, and full of poisonous and rapturous enchantment—was kneaded into what, only a week or two before, had been a lump of wet clay from the Tiber. Soon, apotheosized in an indestructible material, she would be one of the images that men keep forever, finding a heat in them which does not cool down, throughout the centuries.

Another immortal symbol of complexity is the Laocoon group, "which, in its immortal agony, impressed Kenyon as a type of the long, fierce struggle of man, involved in the knotted entanglements of Error and Evil, those two snakes, which, if no divine help intervene, will be sure to strangle him and his children in the end." Human complexity is real and is not to be passed over. The "knotted entanglement" exists, tempered by the simplicity of the divine. Hawthorne portrays the entanglement and dilemma, and its palliation, without venturing beyond the boundaries into preachment or prophecy.

# XIV

## *Hawthorne's Heaven and Earth*

HAWTHORNE imagines paradise in two related ways: as the Garden of Eden or as the lovers in the Garden. In his "Old Manse" essay, prefixed to the *Mosses from an Old Manse* volume, he describes himself and his bride as a new Adam and Eve and identifies the Manse and its grounds as Eden. Heaven is either nature idealized ("Each tree and rock, and every blade of grass, is distinctly imaged, and, however unsightly in reality, assumes ideal beauty in the reflection. . . . All the sky glows downward at our feet: the rich clouds float through the unruffled bosom of the stream like heavenly thoughts through a peaceful heart."), or it is an ideal human love and harmony. Visitors to the Manse find a spell cast over them. "Others could give them pleasure and amusement or instruction—these could be picked up anywhere; but it was for me to give them rest—rest in a life of trouble. What better could be done for those weary and world-worn spirits?"

After Eden follows soon the Fall. The Garden is no permanent dwelling. In rainy weather "Eve's bower in paradise must have been but a cheerless and aguish kind of shelter. . . . The idea of sleeping on a couch of wet roses!" Heaven disappears, for "The usually mirrored surface of the river was blurred by an infinity of raindrops"; and as for Hawthorne himself, "Providence took me by the hand, and—an oddity of dispensation which, I trust, there is no irreverence at smiling at—has led me ... from the Old Manse into a custom house." So heaven is real and is imaged in life, but only momentarily. The world of Hawthorne's fiction is a fallen world, with transient gleams from the sun of divinity.

The Fall in Hawthorne is a fall from harmony to discord, from fellowship to isolation. This isolation is caused by man's doing too much or too little: by thinking himself too good or too bad. There are both positive and negative sinners. Among those who sin positively are priests, fanatics of all kinds, artists, scientists, physicians, and scholars. Any man, in fact, who sets himself a goal, whether of holiness or hard cash, is likely to fall into evil. The materialists waver on the edge of this classification: they are halfway between positive and negative gracelessness.

The positive sinners are too much set on heaven, an ideal, or simply an occupation. Thus there are the over-righteous priests, like Arthur Dimmesdale on the one hand, or Mr. Wilson on the other. Dimmesdale is by nature a true priest of the human heart, but he falls from trying to live like the saint on earth his congregation supposes him to be. He refuses to admit his human fallibility. His real power lies in his sympathy with the erring human heart, but this he attempts to suppress. Significantly, we hear Dimmesdale's great election-day sermon through Hester Prynne, who stands so far from the speaker that she hears only the "music," not the words. What she hears is "a loud or low expression of anguish,—the whisper, or the shriek, as it might be conceived, of suffering humanity, that touched a sensibility in every bosom!" Mr. Wilson, an older colleague of Dimmesdale's, has cultivated his intellect at the expense of his naturally "kind and genial spirit," until "he looked like the darkly engraved portraits which we see prefixed to old volumes of sermons; and had no more right than one of those portraits would have to step forth . . . and meddle with a question of human guilt, passion, and anguish." By suppression Dimmesdale's heart has been perverted; the Reverend Mr. Wilson has no heart left. In this same class of sinners are the religious fanatics: Catharine, the Quaker of "The Gentle Boy," and Richard Digby, the hermit "Man of Adamant." Catharine is isolated by pride and persecution from human love and sins against her neglected son, the gentle boy. Digby sees salvation only in the dark cave of Calvinism, where he is petrified.

There are two kinds of artists in Hawthorne, which may be distinguished as the poet and the novelist. The poet is generally a Romantic idealist: like the priest his eyes are too much set on heaven, but he is treated more gently than the priest because he has fewer pretensions. His function is to remind us that heaven exists by showing us visions of it. In himself he presents the familiar Romantic paradox of the fool of genius, the visionary who is literally "not much good on earth." To go to another writer, the extreme in this type is crazy Pip, Melville's black cabin boy in *Moby Dick*, whose madness is the wisdom of the gods. The transcendental "artist of the beautiful," Ernest, the poet of "The Great Stone Face," and the child of "The Chimaera" in *A Wonder-Book*, are of this family. The last of these "took higher flights upon the aerial steed than ever did Bellerophon, and achieved more honorable deeds than his friend's victory over the Chimaera."

The other artist, the novelist, runs greater dangers. His temptation is to analyze without love and thus violate the sanctity of the human heart. Such an artist is Ethan Brand, and such is the painter of "The Prophetic Pictures":

Like all other men around whom an engrossing purpose wreathes itself, he was insulated from the mass of human kind. . . . Though gentle in manner and upright in intent and action, he did not possess kindly feelings; his heart was cold; no living creature could be brought near enough to keep him warm.

Such also is Miles Coverdale, who struggles against his inclination to become "a spiritualized Paul Pry." Hawthorne is both these artists, poet and novelist, but critics have generally seen the second in him and paid too little attention to the Romantic poet, who may not have fallen at all.

Scientists, physicians, and scholars, like the novelist, sin from a disproportioned bump of intellectual curiosity, which makes them forget their more human purposes. Aylmer, the pure scientist of "The Birthmark," is punished least of these because of his genuine idealism, which makes him almost a poet. His mistake was in marrying. The idealist who understands his own isolation, like Owen Warland, and is prepared to abide by it generally does pretty well. Hawthorne's "empirics," his doctors, are damned because their curiosity has made them forget that they are healers. They have come to look upon human beings as ingenious physical machines which exist mainly to be tinkered with. The pure scholar, like Fanshawe of Hawthorne's earliest novel, cannot live in the common world. Nor does he, like the poet, have a use which redeems him in turning our eyes toward heaven. Fanshawe is permitted to save the heroine—a better chance than scholars have in most novels, it should be remarked. But he is well advised not to marry her, and his early death seems a happy solution.

Many tears were shed over his grave; but the thoughtful and the wise, though turf never covered a nobler heart, could not lament that it was so soon at rest. He left a world for which he was unfit; and we trust, that, among the innumerable stars of heaven, there is one where he has found happiness.

The pure scholar runs the risk of becoming a very impure scholar if he lingers to take his chances. He turns into a perverted idealist. Septimius Felton confuses time with eternity by seeking the magical elixir of life. Life is too short to pursue his studies, so he perverts them to the search for a way to lengthen them. This scholar is a Faust.

The negative sinners are those who are too much set on earth and are themselves mere lumps of earth. These have limited interests or no interests at all. The ambitious materialists are on the border line between positive and negative sin. Judge Pyncheon is a large figure because of the magnitude of his desires, but in his case magnitude is grossness. The shrewd and handsome Westervelt is powerful but soulless. He has a glittering shell with nothing inside it. Hawthorne is unsuccessful with the grasping and cynical materialists because of lack of sympathy with them. Their urges and temptations are not his; their cosmos is too small. Characters like these can fall into evil—Pyncheon and Westervelt bear the marks of the devil—since the soul cannot live as a vacuum. If good is absent, evil will fill its place.

There are those who hardly live at all, since they never grasp any reality. Gervayse Hastings, of "The Christmas Banquet," is isolated in a void. This outwardly fortunate man is inwardly a mere vapor:

"It is a chilliness—a want of earnestness—a feeling as if what should be my heart were a thing of vapor—a haunting perception of unreality! Thus seeming to possess all that other men have—all that men aim at—I have really possessed nothing, neither joys nor griefs. All things, all persons . . . have been like shadows flickering on the wall. It was so with my wife and children—with those who seemed my friends: it is so with yourselves, whom I see now before me. Neither have I myself any real existence, but am a shadow like the rest."

Then there is the keeper of "A Virtuoso's Collection," which contains such curiosities as Peter Schlemihl's shadow and Peter Rugg, the missing man. The virtuoso is the Wandering Jew, frozen beneath the mass of earthly life, so that his touch seems like ice. The optimists of "The Celestial Railway" are, in the same fashion if for different reasons, dead to moral reality. Mr. Smooth-it-away considers that modern conveniences can achieve anything, including heaven. The luggage of sin which Bunyan's pilgrims carried painfully on their backs is now simply checked to the baggage car.

Cold, dull creatures like Wakefield, or Giovanni Guasconti in "Rappaccini's Daughter," sin from triviality and lack of imagination. In "Wakefield" a husband pretends to disappear, his motive being curiosity to see how his wife will take it. She shows a decent grief, but the experiment is disappointing at that. The point is, however, that Wakefield's joke is fatal; he can never return. "He had contrived, or rather he had happened, to dissever himself from the world—to vanish—to give up his place and privileges with living men, without being admitted among the dead." If he should try to go back in actuality he would only learn what he has lost. "Stay, Wakefield! Would you go to the sole home that is left you? Then step into your grave!" Giovanni, likewise, falls into sin from triviality. Despite his "quick Southern fancy" he has no real feeling for Beatrice Rappaccini, which might have saved him.

Then there are earthlings who fall toward the pit by their own weight. These are keepers of fires, earth-demons, and gnomes. Of these one group can be redeemed, usually by the love of a woman, so that they are drawn upwards into a harmony and wholeness of life, resting softly in Abraham's bosom. Such men are Danforth, the blacksmith of "The Artist of the Beautiful," and the more complicated Hollingsworth, of *The Blithedale Romance*. They have a sturdy strength, symbolized by the blacksmith's blows upon metal. As keepers of the fire they are close to life's center, the heart. The heart has its evils, however. Hell fire is tended by such half-human brutes as Bartram the limeburner, of "Ethan Brand," and the earth-fiend Aminadab, the stoker of "The Birthmark": these cannot sink any lower. Some women, some children, and perhaps some artists are unfallen. The children—the gentle boy and Little Joe, the son of Bartram—seem refugees from paradise. They are not likely to stay long on earth. Hawthorne's women have three sources of strength. They have a saving portion of heaven within them; they are supported by human tradition and custom; and they are seldom tempted from the central path. Hester Prynne is seduced by passion and wanders far before she finds her way; the gorgeous Zenobia unsexes herself and throws away her natural armor; Catharine the Quaker is led away from her womanly responsibilities, and Dorothy Pearson takes them up from her. Phoebe Pyncheon is the embodiment of the central tradition of the heart, while the more ethereal Hilda of *The Marble Faun* is buoyed by heaven. Some artists, like the artist of the beautiful, perhaps escape the fall by retaining a primal freshness of sensibility. They do not, however, escape isolation. They are less fortunate in this respect than the women. Action itself brings evil, and Hawthorne's women do not have to act.

Most thoughtful critics of Hawthorne have found unresolved conflicts in both his life and his works, and they have generally seen in him more darkness than light. Malcolm Cowley says that "the stories reflected a conflict between his instincts and his reasoned convictions." He remarks of Hawthorne's character:

Everywhere . . . one finds a sort of doubleness. . . . He was cold and sensuous, sluggish and active, radical and conservative, and a visionary with a hard sense of money values. These contradictions, these inner tensions, lend force to his stories and make their author an endless study.

Newton Arvin finds in him more interest in evil than in good. To Hawthorne "guilt and wrong . . . are terribly deeply meshed in the texture of human experience . . . his sense of the depths to which they can fall, of the maze of error in which they can wander, was steady and fascinated."

I do not quote these passages to refute them, but to put the case differently. Certainly these complications are the sources of Hawthorne's power and his continued fascination. And when darkness and light exist together the dark will always seem to win—it is so perfectly in keeping with our fears. Dark and light, however, are equally important in Hawthorne—that is the way he wants them. He is simply the most hardheaded and unillusioned of all writers, and his motto is, "Render unto Caesar that which is Caesar's, and unto God that which is God's." Hawthorne is a dualist of good and evil and of heaven and earth. Like Melville he is more Manichaean than most theologies would approve. For him, as for Melville, "the tortoise is both dark and bright"; but Hawthorne has not Melville's urge to struggle.

It must be emphasized that there is no synthesis in Hawthorne's thinking, only thesis and antithesis in balance. He reacted against the easy and optimistic solutions of liberalism and Emersonian transcendentalism, which left out some of the pieces in order to put the puzzle together. His only reconciliation is acceptance of life's differences and contradictions. The solution he offers is the moral at the end of "The Birthmark": heaven exists and earth exists—accept your human imperfections, and wait. The lot of man is "care and sorrow, and troubled joy," but there is perfection elsewhere. Life is heaven, and earth—and neither of these can be ignored. This theme in itself might seem a solution. The difficulty is, however, that man wants heaven immediately. This irrational desire he cannot master, but can only hold in check at best.

Balance in Hawthorne's writing always involves sacrifice. To achieve one good, another must be abandoned. In his psychology the head and the heart can never be in harmony, and no character can be complete. Where the materials for synthesis exist, as in *The House of the Seven Gables*, and "The Maypole of Merry Mount," we find only an unequal compromise. Holgrave, the daring head, will have to sacrifice to live with Phoebe, the conservative heart; and Phoebe will receive nothing which she does not already possess. The Lord and Lady of the May will get along with the Puritans chiefly by giving in to them.

The apparent gloom of Hawthorne's work is explicable in two ways. First, his belief in heaven is so strong that he can easily afford to be interested in the complexities of the merely human. With a fixed star to guide him, he can wander in safety along the dark paths of human confusion and error. He can involve Beatrice Rappaccini in difficulties too great for human help because there is help for her elsewhere. In the end, the balance will always be righted. Second, there is what we know but tend always to forget: the simple need of a writer to make his stories interesting. The dark is better material than the light. All action is imperfection, and all plots are about something that has gone wrong, set over against a norm of rightness by which we judge them. Hawthorne's darkness has the structural and dramatic value of contrast. There is a third possible reason for his gloom, but this can only be guessed at. Having evolved a deliberately modest and cautious system, did Hawthorne find that it failed to satisfy him? Did he himself upset the balance?

For Hawthorne, heaven is eternity, certainty, perfection, spirit; earth is time, ambiguity, imperfection, matter. The contrast is pervasive in his fiction, but I shall present it here chiefly in lesser-known tales and in the unfinished romances of "the last phase" of Hawthorne's career, to avoid retracing steps already taken in earlier chapters. The symbolism is simple and central. Heaven is light, order, a fixed star, a fountain; earth is a veil, darkness, a cracked marble, the departing year. The two are contrasted as the light and the veil, as the uniting of eternity and time, as plan and procession. The delusion of heaven is a false light against the true, the unlawful elixir of life against the ever-flowing fountain.

The minister's black veil shuts out the light of eternity. On his deathbed he is urged to cast it aside at last:

"Venerable Father Hooper, . . . the moment of your release is at hand. Are you ready for the lifting of the veil that shuts in time from eternity? . . ."

"Yea," said he, in faint accents, "my soul hath a patient weariness until that veil be lifted. . . ."

"Before the veil of eternity be lifted, let me cast aside this veil from your face!"

But the minister refuses to permit the removal of the veil, and goes into his grave with his face still concealed. While his colleague would merge time and eternity by the symbolic act of throwing off the veil, Father Hooper by his refusal holds them inexorably separate. " 'Never!' cried the veiled clergyman. 'On earth, never!' "

"Night Sketches," the description of a walk through the streets of a New England town, contains darkness and several kinds of light. The dark is a veil which hides the sky "as though heaven and all its lights were blotted from the system of the universe." The faint light of earth gives little assistance. "A lamp is burning dimly at the distant corner, and throws just enough of light along the street to show and exaggerate by so faintly showing the perils and difficulties which beset my path." The light of human reason, then, is dim in the darkness of reality. Perhaps it is even illusory, for this light gives way to the bright lights of the shopping district. "Methinks the scene is an emblem of the deceptive glare which mortals throw around their footsteps in the moral world, thus bedazzling themselves till they forget the impenetrable obscurity that hems them in, and that can be dispelled only by radiance from above." The true light, the lamp of faith, is not to be found in the center but on the outskirts of town. It is imaged in a matter-of-fact tin lantern, carried by a solitary figure who "passes fearlessly into the unknown gloom, whither I will not follow him." This lantern, "kindled at the fireside of his home, will light him back to that same fireside again," which in its steadfastness is like the light of heaven. "And thus we, night wanderers through a stormy and dismal world, if we bear the lamp of Faith, enkindled at a celestial fire, it will surely lead us home to that heaven whence its radiance was borrowed."

In "The Wedding Knell," as in "The Minister's Black Veil," men confuse heaven with earth, eternity with time. An aged couple would marry, but the time is past for such vanities. The church bell tolls as for a funeral. The bridegroom appears in a shroud, an objectification which shocks the bride into recognizing the truth. She gives up her hopes of earthly joy. " 'My life is gone in vanity and emptiness. But at its close there is one true feeling. It has made me what I was in youth; it makes me worthy of you. Time is no more for both of us. Let us wed for Eternity!' " The wedding proceeds, and as it does so the tolling bell is drowned out by the peal of the organ, a symbol of the triumph of eternity.

Emblems of time which yet evoke eternity are the personifications of "The Sister Years." The scene is the Salem City Hall, the time is midnight of December 31, 1838; the characters are the Old and the New Year. The hope of the newcomer balances the pessimism of the year going out.

"Alas for you, then, my poor sister!" said the Old Year, sighing, as she uplifted her burden. "We, grandchildren of Time, are born to trouble. Happiness, they say, dwells in the mansions of Eternity; but we can only lead mortals thither, step by step, with reluctant murmurings, and ourselves must perish on the threshold."

As the New Year steps confidently into the streets, she is assailed by the taint of mortality breathing in the night air. There can be no lifting of the doom of earth. "But there were millions left alive to rejoice at her coming; and so she pursued her way with confidence, strewing emblematic flowers."

Some tales and sketches objectify earth as a procession and heaven as its plan or organizing principle. In "David Swan" a young man turns aside to sleep by the edge of a busy highway. "While he lay sound asleep in the shade, other people were wide awake, and passed to and fro, afoot, on horseback, and in all sorts of vehicles, along the sunny road by his bedchamber." The sleeper is not independent of the procession of life, although he has dropped out of it. He lies passively at the mercy of its chances. Prosperity, love, and death brush closely by him in the persons of a rich Boston couple who are tempted to adopt him, a pretty girl who is attracted by his looks, and a pair of thieves who consider murdering him. Finally the sleeper wakes, and takes up his place in the procession once more. The flow of life, capricious as it seems, is controlled by an organizing principle. "Does it not argue a superintending Providence that, while viewless and unexpected events thrust themselves continually athwart our path, there should still be regularity enough in mortal life to render foresight even partially available?" Note that this is a measured and cautious conclusion, in which "viewless and unexpected events" are at least as influential as regularity and foresight.

In "The Toll-Gatherer's Day" life is the daily procession of men and vehicles which passes over a toll-bridge. All day the toll-gatherer watches it. With evening the procession ceases, and the old man turns his eyes seaward to a lighthouse and the stars above it. The stars are "kindling in the sky, as if but a little way beyond; and mingling reveries of heaven with remembrances of earth, the whole procession of mortal travellers, all the dusty pilgrimage which he has witnessed, seems like a flitting show of phantoms for his thoughtful soul to muse upon." Heaven is imminent in the stars and the lighthouse, symbols of certainty and reassurance; and by their light the memory of the procession is merely "a flitting show of phantoms." Yet the procession is real in the daytime, when stars and lighthouses do not shine.

"The Procession of Life" deals with a parade under a chief marshal. In this parade all men have their places, but "its members are classified by the merest external circumstances." Discarding distinctions of rank and wealth, Hawthorne would reorganize his procession on the basis of intellectual ability. This, he thinks, is an improvement but is not sufficient. Next, he would divide his marchers into good men and evil. Better, but still not good enough. For our judgments are bounded and relative; all earthly standards, in fact, are vain. There is no help in the marshal, for the marshal is Death, who must at last desert us by the wayside; and he "knows not, more than we, our destined goal." Yet there is a goal which faith can at least dimly perceive. "God, who made us, knows, and will not leave us on our toilsome and doubtful march, either to wander in infinite uncertainty, or perish by the way!" Earth, then, has only an illusion of order which vanishes as the mind attempts to probe it. The trusted marshal, magnificent on his white horse, is Death. But in heaven the true order appears, and in place of the marshal is God.

In "Main Street" the road itself is an emblem of permanence, since its outlines remain unaltered through the changes of centuries. "Main Street" is a historical sketch in which more than two hundred years of New England life are focused by the chief thoroughfare of Salem. Hawthorne calls this procession of life a "shifting panorama," which could be embodied in a puppet show. The exhibition will require "a multitude of puppets" and great variety in the lighting, but the scene will be constant throughout. Scene and street have the order of heaven; the remainder is the shadow play of life on earth.

The elixir of life and the fountain are the false and the true emblems of heaven. The quasi-magical elixir symbolizes a fatal confusion between heaven and earth. In "Dr. Heidegger's Experiment" the doctor allows three old friends to drink the waters of the Fountain of Youth, a flask of which he has opportunely received from Florida. In this story the effect of the elixir is only mo-

mentary; even so, it is disquieting. The subjects are el-
derly voluptuaries, to whom age has meant despair. Re-
stored a few seconds to youth, they quickly demonstrate
that experience has taught them nothing.

The elixir of life is a theme in three of the four unfinished romances of Hawthorne's last years. It is hinted
at in *Dr. Grimshawe's Secret,* while it is overt and important in *The Dolliver Romance* and *Septimius Felton.*
*The Dolliver Romance,* although the shortest of the unfinished novels, is complete in terms of the time-eternity
opposition. Dr. Dolliver is a forlorn old apothecary,
whose only hold on life is his responsibility to his or-
phaned granddaughter. He experiences an unaccountable
sense of well-being after taking a mysterious cordial
which he himself has compounded for an unknown customer who never came back for it. All its ingredients
but one are familiar to the doctor, but the one he has
never been able to trace.

The dose, first taken by accident, brings about a "happy condition of his spirits and physical energies." It decidedly improves his vision, lending to his eyes an "unaccustomed gleaming brightness." The effect of the cordial is favorable, then, although evil is suggested in the
hint about the eyes. But Dolliver is visited by Colonel
Dabney, a wealthy fellow-townsman. After incompre-
hensibly threatening the old man the Colonel demands
the cordial, which he drains in one gulp. The results are
remarkable:

The Colonel sat a moment in his chair, panting for breath;
then started to his feet with a prompt vigor that contrasted
widely with the infirm and rheumatic movements that had
hitherto characterized him. He struck his forehead violently

with one hand, and smote his chest with the other: he stamped his foot thunderously on the ground; then he leaped up to the ceiling, and came down with an elastic bound. Then he laughed, a wild, exulting ha! ha! with a strange triumphant roar that filled the house and reechoed through it; a sound full of fierce, animal rapture,—enjoyment of sensual life mixed up with a sort of horror. After all, real as it was, it was like the sounds a man makes in a dream. And this, while the potent draught seemed still to be making its way through his system. . . . Finally, he uttered a loud unearthly screech, in the midst of which his voice broke, as if some unseen hand were throttling him, and, starting forward, he fought frantically, as if he would clutch the life that was being rent away,—and fell forward with a dead thump upon the floor.

The cordial is the elixir of life. Dolliver has drunk it in safety because, first, he has limited himself to a drop at a time, following the directions left by his unknown customer. Second, he has drunk in innocence, unaware of the cordial's significance. Third, his motives have been unselfish; he has wished to live long enough to provide for his granddaughter. Finding himself the better for his treatment, he has naturally continued it. Colonel Dabney, however, is a different matter. With full knowledge of the cordial's purpose, he has confused eternity and time. He has sought an eternal life of sensual enjoyment and power. Dolliver escapes on condition that he shall drink no more of the false water of life. The unfortunate Dabney has drunk the remainder of the cordial. The only alternative open to Dolliver is to discover the unknown ingredient; and we know, though Dolliver does not, that it has been destroyed. It came from a poisonous shrub, a specimen of which had actually been in his garden; and this specimen, symbolically enough, has been uprooted by his grandchild at play.

The most notable effect in *The Dolliver Romance* is the physical impact of time. The opening scene, in which Dolliver is introduced, is chill with images of senility. The doctor is "a worthy person of extreme antiquity," with "locks of silvery white hair" and "a meagre and duskily yellow visage." Getting up in the morning is a serious ordeal to him. His bed curtains are faded, his furniture crazed; even the gilt serpent which is his sign of business is eaten up with dry rot. The cordial rouses him to a dim consciousness of "an unfrozen drop of youthfulness, somewhere within him." So heavy a stress upon the ravages of time is clearly intended to heighten the theme of earthly immortality by emphasizing the weight of the temporal burden.

The hero of *Septimius Felton* commits the same error as Colonel Dabney, although from higher motives. Hawthorne's attitude is stated early in the book. The student Septimus has a sense

that he, at least, might never die. The feeling was not peculiar to Septimius. It is an instinct, the meaning of which is mistaken. We have strongly within us the sense of an undying principle, and we transfer that true sense to this life and to the body, instead of interpreting it justly as the promise of spiritual immortality.

Septimius has a Faustian craving for infinite knowledge and power. Against his urge for eternal life Hawthorne opposes the monotonous horror of physical permanence: "What a worn and ugly thing one of these fresh little blades of grass would seem if it were not to fade and wither in its time, after being green in its time."

From the first the elixir is associated with death. Septimius learns the formula from a dying man, whom he himself has shot in fair fight. The victim, a young British officer (the time is 1775), is superbly fitted to enjoy this world: "Had he been gifted with permanence on earth, there could not have been a more admirable creature than this young man." It is therefore important that his death is a reconciliation, even a triumph.

What a change had come over it since, only a few moments ago, he looked at that death-contorted countenance! Now there was a high and sweet expression upon it, of great joy and surprise, and yet a quietude diffused throughout, as if the peace being so very great was what had surprised him. The expression was like a light gleaming and glowing within him.

As in *The Dolliver Romance* one ingredient is missing from the formula, and as in *The Dolliver Romance* this ingredient is noxious. It comes from a flower which grows only in the soil of graves, the gorgeous but unnatural *sanguinea sanguinissima*. An old legend hints that the flower of immortality will prosper only if planted on a fresh grave of bloody death. As Septimius pursues the secret, a manuscript comes to his hands of one who was fabled to have discovered it; but the manuscript itself is subtly poisonous,

the expression of an intellect originally greatly gifted and capable of high things, but gone utterly astray, partly by its own subtlety, partly by yielding to the temptations of the lower part of its own nature, by yielding the spiritual to a keen sagacity of lower things, until it was quite fallen; and yet fallen in such a way, that it seemed not only to itself, but to mankind, not fallen at all, but wise and good, and fulfilling all the ends of intellect in such a life as ours, and proving, moreover, that earthly life was good, and all that the development of our nature demanded.

The directions set forth in this manuscript suggest that the conditions of earthly immortality are somewhat ironical. (It might be interesting to compare *Septimius Felton* with Aldous Huxley's *After Many a Summer Dies the Swan*.) To live forever one must live as little as possible, suppressing emotion, husbanding energy, standing aside from action.

Septimius at last produces the magic elixir. The conclusion is an ironic reversal. He has been deluded: the flower of life was a flower of death, "a baneful growth out of a grave," and the water of life is a deadly poison. The meaning is plain. Such a search, with what it involves in mind and spirit, must always end in disaster. The elixir appears in other Hawthorne tales. In "The Birthmark" the potion which Aylmer distills to treat his wife is a liquor "colorless as water, but bright enough to be the draught of immortality." In erasing the birthmark the elixir also causes her death, for perfection and earth cannot mingle. The elixir fallacy occurs in different symbolism in "The Gentle Boy," "The Hall of Fantasy," and "The Lily's Quest."

The fountain is the true water of eternal life. This symbol appears early (and a little unexpectedly) in "A Rill from the Town Pump." On the spot where the pump now stands was originally a bubbling spring, whose water was "as bright and clear, and deemed as precious, as liquid diamonds." Of this spring drank the Indians, then the Puritans. "Thus, one generation after another was consecrated to Heaven by its waters, and cast their waxing and waning shadows into its glassy bosom, and vanished from the earth, as if mortal life were but an image in a fountain." The spring disappeared from sight, "but, in the course of time, a Town Pump was sunk into the source of the ancient spring; and when the first decayed, another took its place—and then another, and still another. . . ." The original rill flows on, an emblem of permanence in change.

In "Egotism; or, The Bosom Serpent" there is also a fountain of eternity. Roderick Elliston, the man who carries the serpent in his breast, reclines by a fountain which is "born at every moment, yet of an age coeval with the rocks, and far surpassing the venerable antiquity of a forest." There is a legend of a snake which lurked within this fountain, "pure and innocent as it looks," and Roderick speculates half-fancifully whether the serpent in his bosom may not be the same. He is freed from the snake by the touch of his betrothed Rosina: "At that moment, if report be trustworthy, the sculptor [Roderick's companion] beheld a waving motion through the grass, and heard a tinkling sound, as if something had plunged into the fountain." Rosina interprets, with the insight of love: "The serpent was but a dark fantasy, and what it typified was as shadowy as itself. The past, dismal as it seems, shall fling no gloom upon the future. To give it its due importance we must think of it but as an anecdote in our eternity." The snake is an evil limited by time, which vanishes into eternity. Reconciliation consists in a clear understanding of the qualities that belong to each.

232

In "The Man of Adamant" the true waters of life are rejected through blindness. The gloomy Richard Digby withdraws to a cave in search of his soul's salvation. Near the cavern's mouth stands a fountain, which Digby ignores. He drinks instead the water which trickles from the roof of the cave: water which "seemed to possess the power of converting what it bathed to stone." The spirit of his dead love pleads with him to drink from the fountain: " 'I pray thee, by thy hope of heaven, and as thou wouldst not dwell in this tomb forever, drink of this hallowed water, be it but a single drop!' " But Digby refuses and dies. His body petrifies, and he becomes "a man of adamant." He has mistaken the false waters for the true, which love would have shown him.

The fountain plays some part in *Fanshawe* and in "The Intelligence Office," among others; but one more example is sufficient. I cannot resist the peculiar appropriateness of the fountain in "Rappaccini's Daughter." With its complement the shrub, it stands in the center of the garden:

There was the ruin of a marble fountain in the centre, sculptured with rare art, but so wofully shattered that it was impossible to trace the original design from the chaos of remaining fragments. The water, however, continued to gush and sparkle into the sunbeams as cheerfully as ever. A little gurgling sound ascended . . . as if a fountain were an immortal spirit that sung its song unceasingly and without heeding the vicissitudes around it, while one century embodied it in marble and another scattered the perishable garniture on the soil.

The flowing water is eternity, the shattered marble is time. The elements of the symbol are clearly dual. The shrub is monistic in its organic growth and its inextricable confusion of good and evil. It is glowingly beautiful, but deadly poisonous. Its brightness and its luxuriance are so excessive that they seem unnatural. The shrub, in fact, is the false flower of life, the gorgeous *sanguinea sanguinissima* which grows in the soil of graves. The fountain and the shrub are both emblems for Beatrice Rappaccini. The shrub is the false Beatrice, the noxious prodigy of Rappaccini's invention; the fountain is the true Beatrice, her perishable body and her immortal soul. The shrub must die, for its complexities could never be explicated. Thus Hawthorne, while refusing to provide a natural or human solution, balances his tragic earth with a clear vision of heaven.

# Index

Achilles: 197
Acrasia: 102
Adams, Richard: 113
Addison, Joseph: 124
*After Many a Summer Dies the Swan*: 231
Allegory: 7, 41–42, 100, 104, 105
Ambiguity: as doubt, 11, 21–22; as picturesque, 10, 21, 53, 58; as play, 11–12; as tragedy, 13, 21–22; as truth, 10–11, 12
Archer, Isabel: 10
Archimago: 101
Aristotle: 197
Armida: 102
Arvin, Newton: 219–20

Balzac, Honoré de: 41
Blake, William: 88
Brook Farm: 168
Brooks, Cleanth: 119
Brownell, William Crary: 53
Bunthorne: 171
Bunyan, John: 182, 217
Byron, George Gordon, Lord: 77

Carr, John Dickson: 101
Chaucer, Geoffrey: 41
Cimabue: 210
Coleridge, Samuel Taylor: 32, 59, 68, 112, 117, 119, 207, 209
Conrad, Joseph: 10

Cowley, Malcolm: 219

Dickens, Charles: 3
*Don Juan*: 28
Dreiser, Theodore: 4

Eliot, T. S.: 7, 197
Emerson, Ralph Waldo: 131

*Faerie Queene, The:* 7, 101
"Fall of the House of Usher, The": 101, 162
Faulkner, William: 4
Faust: 216
Fielding, Henry: 5, 41
*Form and Fable in American Fiction*: 108
Fourierism: 169
Fra Angelico: 197, 199

Giotto: 210
Guido: 197, 199

Hawthorne, Julian: 5
Hawthorne, Nathaniel: abstractness in, 31–32, 149; acceptance in, 7, 90; aesthetic design in, 8–9, 22–32, 39–40, 47ff., 62ff., 138ff., 169–70, 189, 221; allegory in, 7, 22ff., 41ff., 59ff.; allegory and symbol in, 59ff.; aloofness in, 5, 22, 31–32, 103, 149; ambiguity in, 4, 5, 10–13, 15ff.,

35ff., 105, 106, 113, 117, 122, 124, 139–55; balance in, 22, 24, 25, 28, 30, 35–36, 103, 184–85, 221–22; clarity in, 4, 13, 22–32, 105, 145, 234; complexity in, 4, 9–10, 13, 33ff., 53, 54, 96ff., 171ff., 192ff., 234; conception of science of, 127; detachment of, 118, 119; dualism in, 4, 5–6, 14, 32, 219ff., 233–34; gloom in, 119; humor in, 105, 106, 118–19, 148–49; irony in, 13, 22, 23, 24, 28, 31, 32, 40, 47, 48, 55, 102–103, 105–106, 109, 115, 118, 119, 131, 138–42, 151–52, 160; philosophy of, 5–6; reconciliation in, 7, 32, 52, 64, 68–69; Romanticism in, 76–78, 120, 123, 188, 214; sensibility of, 125; setting in, 8–9, 19–20, 24, 27, 30, 43, 46–47, 49–52, 173; simplicity in, 3–4, 22ff., 33ff., 46, 50, 96ff., 192ff.; spiritual levels in, 43–44, 61–62, 86, 135–38; structural rhythm in, 107; texture and richness in, 120; tone in, 4–5, 28–32, 35, 65, 67, 102–103, 119, 138, 144, 148–49, 154, 189; use of color in, 25, 26, 51, 67, 97, 133–34

Hawthorne, characters:
Aminadab, 6, 85, 218
Aylmer, 6, 7, 85, 117ff., 215, 231
Dr. Baglioni, 85, 92, 97, 100
Bartram, 44ff., 85, 218
Bellerophon, 188, 214
Brand, Ethan, 7, 43ff., 85, 100, 157, 160, 187, 215
Goodman Brown, 15ff., 105, 126
Chillingworth, 9, 126, 132ff., 160

Catharine the Quaker, 214, 219
Goody Cloyse, 17ff.
Coverdale, Miles, 88, 169ff., 182–86, 187ff., 215
The Cynic, 82
Colonel Dabney, 227–29
Danforth, Robert, 70ff., 83–85, 86ff., 124, 218
Digby, Richard, 214, 233
Dimmesdale, Arthur, 80, 126, 132ff., 166, 213–14
Dr. Dolliver, 227–29
Donatello, 10, 80, 125, 137, 190, 192–95, 199ff.
Elizabeth, 6, 34–35, 36, 37, 38
Elliston, Roderick, 232
Endicott, John, 8–9, 60–61, 62, 67
Ernest, 214
Faith, 15ff.
Fanshawe, 215–16
Fauntleroy, 173–74, 176
Felton, Septimius, 85, 86, 216, 229–31
Foster, Silas, 82–83
Garfield, Rose, 86
Georgiana, 117ff.
Giovanni, 91ff., 108, 126, 128, 217, 218
Deacon Gookin, 18ff.
Hagburn, Robert, 85, 86
Hastings, Gervayse, 217
Mistress Hibbins, 144
Hilda, 190, 191, 196–202, 204
Holgrave, 151, 153, 154, 156–58, 163ff., 168, 221
Hollingsworth, 169, 178–82, 184ff., 218
Father Hooper, 33ff., 222
Hovenden, Annie, 70ff., 85–86
Hovenden, Peter, 70ff., 73–75, 79, 80, 81–83, 87
Ilbrahim, 188, 218

# Index

The Jew of Nuremberg, 47, 49, 53, 58

Kenyon, 190, 195, 197ff.

Little Joe, 45–46, 47, 51, 52, 57, 188, 218

The Lord and Lady of the May, 60, 61–62, 64, 66–67, 221

Maule, Matthew, 152, 157

The Maules, 152–53

Miriam, 10, 80, 125, 173, 190, 194ff.

Major Molineux, 104ff.

Old Moodie (*see* Fauntleroy), 176

Pearl, 136–37, 142

Pearson, Dorothy, 86, 219

Priscilla, 82–83, 169ff., 174–76, 179, 180, 181ff., 187–89

Prynne, Hester, 14, 80, 132ff., 213, 219

Pyncheon, Alice, 157, 165

Pyncheon, Clifford, 150, 153, 154, 155, 157ff.

Pyncheon, Hepzibah, 150ff., 154–55ff.

Pyncheon, Judge Jaffrey, 134, 151ff., 158–61, 163, 167, 187, 216, 217

Pyncheon, Phoebe, 3, 86, 150ff., 155, 157, 158, 159, 164, 165, 219, 221

Pyncheons, the, 152–54, 162, 165–67, 193

Rappaccini, 85, 91ff., 126, 129, 160, 234

Rappaccini, Beatrice, 91ff., 108, 117, 218, 234

Robin, 104ff.

Rosina, 232

Mr. Smooth-It-Away, 217

Village Worthies, the, 44–45, 54, 55–56

Wakefield, 217–18

Warland, Owen, 70ff., 128, 215

Westervelt, 82, 137, 160, 169ff., 186–87, 216, 217

Williams, Roger, 8–9

Mr. Wilson, 213–14

Zenobia, 82, 169ff., 173–78, 179ff., 219

"Hawthorne's 'The Birthmark': Science as Religion": 126

Hawthorne, symbols:

Adam and Eve, 14, 61, 99

Arcadia, 170–72, 174, 175, 192, 194, 195, 196, 201, 202

Birthmark, 117ff.

Cavern, the, 14, 84, 178, 179, 180, 233

Day and night, 25–26

Devil, the, 14, 17, 18, 21, 28–29, 30, 31, 106, 140, 187, 217

Eden, 14, 98, 99, 192, 196, 200, 202, 212

Elixir of life, the, 227ff.

Fire, 14, 49–51, 84, 143–44, 178, 180, 218

Fountain, the, 13, 14, 93–94, 226, 231–34

Garden, the (*see* Eden), 13, 14, 93, 94, 96, 97, 98, 99, 101, 102, 138, 164, 212

Golden Age, the, 65, 192, 193, 194, 195, 196, 202

Hearth, the, 14, 84–85

House, the, 162–67

Laughter, 107, 109–11

Moonlight, 107, 112–16

Mouldering corpse, the, 158, 167, 205, 209–10

Paradise, 65, 99, 200, 212

Rome, 202ff.

Serpent, the, 14, 17, 187, 232

Stream, the, 13, 138

Sunlight, 14, 52, 94–95, 134, 142

Town and the forest, the, 14, 25–26, 136, 142, 144

Veil, the, 6, 20, 33ff., 222–23

Vulcan, 14, 84, 178–79

Hawthorne, themes: appearance and reality, 23, 26–27, 87–88, 94–95, 139ff., 158–59, 173–74, 186–87; the artist, 55, 70ff., 213; as novelist, 215; as poet, 214; childhood and maturity, 116; continuity of guilt, 150ff.; detachment and sympathy, 112, 120ff.; the fall of man, 133ff., 190ff., 212–13; the fortunate fall, 132, 191; good and evil, 16, 22, 25, 26–27, 91ff.; the head and the heart, 39–40, 44, 84–85, 136, 155–58, 162, 165, 174–76, 178–82, 183, 187–88, 213–19; heaven, 5, 134–35; heaven and earth, 5–6, 93ff., 135–38, 192, 196ff., 212ff.; hell, 5, 134, 143–44, 187; idealism and materialism, 71ff., 174ff., 186–89; illusion and reality, 112, 113, 123, 124; imagination, 112, 188–89; imagination and understanding, 72ff.; isolation, 44, 47, 89–90, 98, 101, 157, 166, 215–19; materialism, 153ff.; 186–88, 213, 216–17, 230–31; mechanism and organism, 72, 75–76, 207–209; pride, 44, 54, 100, 153, 154; the Puritan, 7, 27, 28–29, 39–40, 60ff., 86, 133, 138, 144, 145, 147–48, 183, 204, 205; radical and conservative, 150ff., 168ff.; secret sin, 6, 31–32, 33ff., 139ff.; shrewdness, 107, 109; time and eternity, 14, 72ff., 93ff., 135, 221ff.; the Unpardonable Sin, 43–44, 47, 49, 157; wandering and nightmare, 106

Hawthorne, titles:

*American Notebooks,* 120

"Artist of the Beautiful, The," 70–90, 218

"Birthmark, The," 6, 117–31, 215, 218, 220, 231

*Blithedale Romance, The,* 12, 82, 137, 160, 168–69

"Celestial Railroad, The," 12–13, 217

"Chimaera, The," 188, 214

"Christmas Banquet, The," 217

"Custom House, The," 4

"David Swan," 224–25

*Dr. Grimshawe's Secret,* 227

"Dr. Heidegger's Experiment," 226–27

*Dolliver Romance, The,* 227–29, 231

"Earth's Holocaust," 125, 156

"Egotism; or, The Bosom Serpent," 232

"Endicott and the Red Cross," 8–9

*English Notebooks, The,* 159

"Ethan Brand," 41–58, 110, 124, 134, 188, 218

*Fanshawe,* 215–16, 233

"Gentle Boy, The," 86, 231

"Gray Champion, The," 12

"Great Carbuncle, The," 82

"Great Stone Face, The," 214

"Hall of Fantasy, The," 231

*House of the Seven Gables, The,* 3, 10–11, 134, 150–67, 168, 174, 193, 221

"Howe's Masquerade," 12

"Intelligence Officer, The," 233

"Legends of the Province House," 12

"Lily's Quest, The," 231

# Index

"Main Street," 226
"Man of Adamant, The," 214, 233
*Marble Faun, The*, 10, 80, 125, 130, 137, 173, 189–211, 219
"Maypole of Merry Mount, The," 59–69, 86–87, 89–90, 221
"Minister's Black Veil, The," 6, 13, 33–40, 222, 223
"Miraculous Pitcher, The," 11
*Masses from an Old Manse*, 212
"My Kinsman, Major Molineux," 104–16, 118
"Night Sketches," 222–23
"Old Manse, The," 212
"Procession of Life, The," 225–26
"Prophetic Pictures, The," 88, 215
"Rappaccini's Daughter," 91–103, 108, 217, 218, 233–34
"Rill From the Town Pump, A," 3, 231–32
*Scarlet Letter, The*, 9, 13–14, 80, 86, 118–19, 124, 132–49, 150, 166
*Septimius Felton*, 227, 229–31
"Sister Years, The," 224
*Tanglewood Tales*, 11
"Toll-Gatherer's Day, The," 225
*Twice-Told Tales*, 12
"Virtuoso's Collection, A," 217
"Wakefield," 217–18
"Wedding Knell, The," 223
*Wonder-Book, A*, 11, 188, 214
"Young Goodman Brown," 12, 13, 15–32, 105, 106, 187

Heilman, Robert: 126, 127, 128
*Hellas*: 168
Hoffman, Daniel G.: 108, 109

Hughes, Richard: 142
Hutchinson, Anne: 145
Huxley, Aldous: 231

*Iliad, The*: 197
*Inferno, The*: 197
*Innocent Voyage, The*: 142
Irony: 103; of situation, 138–42

James, Henry: 4, 10, 53
Jason: 102

Keats, John: 40, 77, 112, 115, 116

Lathrop, George Parsons: 148
"Ligeia": 113
Locke, John: 124
*Lord Jim*: 10

Malbecco: 101
Mannette, Lucie: 3
Marquand, John P.: 3
Matthiessen, F. O.: 11, 16, 156
Maugham, W. Somerset: 3
Medea: 102
Melville, Herman: 4, 59, 124, 214, 220
*Midsummer Night's Dream, A*: 112
Milton, John: 197
*Moby Dick*: 214
Molière: 28
Motley, John Lathrop: 10

"Ode to a Nightingale": 115
*Othello*: 18

*Paradiso, The*: 197
*Pilgrim's Progress, The*: 7, 12, 70
Plato: 197
"Pleasures of Imagination, The": 124

239

Poe, Edgar Allan: 101, 113, 123, 162
*Point of No Return*: 3
*Portrait of a Lady, The*: 10
*Prometheus Unbound*: 125

Ransom, John Crowe: 68
*Rape of the Lock, The*: 41
Raphael: 206
Renaissance, the: 206–207
Roman Catholicism: 203–205, 209, 210
Romanticism: 7, 76–79, 120, 131, 188, 214

Shelley, Percy Bysshe: 77, 125, 168
"Sleeping Beauty": 102, 183
Spenser, Edmund: 41
Stevens, Wallace: 112
Stewart, Randall: 101
Symbolism: 13, 42

*Tale of Two Cities, A*: 3
Tasso: 102
Thackeray, William Makepeace: 4
*Theory of Literature*: 13
Thoreau, Henry David: 172
"Tiger, The": 88
Titian: 206
Trollope, Anthony: 118, 119

*Understanding Fiction*: 119

Van Doren, Mark: 137

Wandering Jew, the: 58, 217
Warren, Austin: 13, 191
Warren, Robert Penn: 119
Wellek, René: 13
"Whiteness of the Whale, The": 124
Whitman, Walt: 131
Winters, Yvor: 11, 16
Wordsworth, William: 77